Heavenly Bites

The Best of Muslim Home Cooking

Karimah bint Dawood

KUBE

Heavenly Bites: The Best of Muslim Home Cooking

First published in England by Kube Publishing Ltd
Markfield Conference Centre
Ratby Lane, Markfield
Leicestershire LE67 9SY
United Kingdom
Tel: +44 (0) 1530 249230
Fax: +44 (0) 1530 249656
Website: www.kubepublishing.com
Email: info@kubepublishing.com

Cataloguing-in-publication data is available from the British Library

ISBN: 978-1-84774-031-1 *paperback*

Photography: Karimah Bint Dawood and Orin Cozier

Cover Design: Fatima Jamadar
Book layout and Typesetting: Nasir Cadir

Printed in Turkey by Imak Ofset

Contents

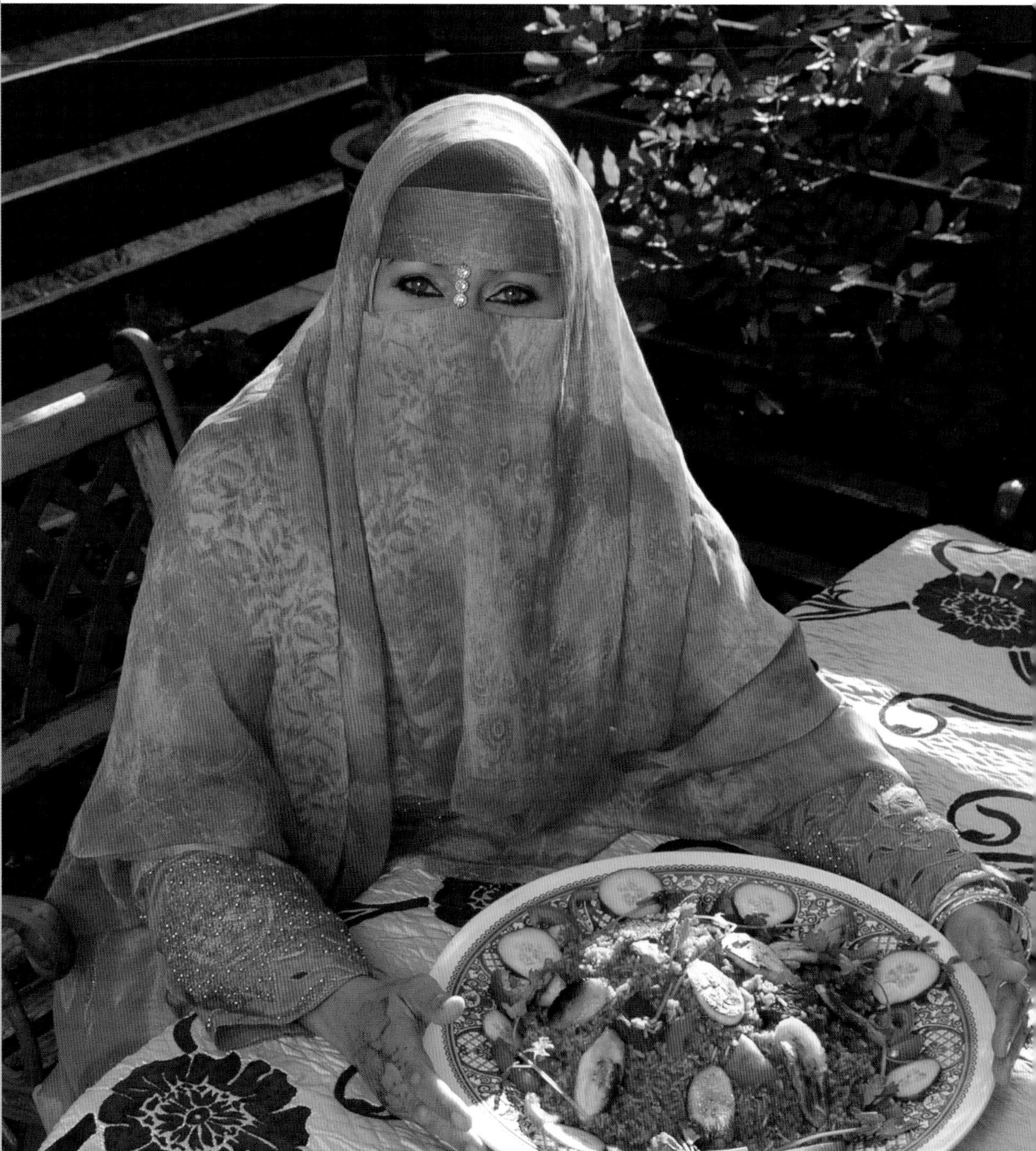

Introduction
Faith and Food

This work is only in your hands by the grace of Allah, and it is really great to be able to present this twenty-first-century eclectic British Muslim menu to you, my beloved readers. It is a personal mix of faith and food, stories and recipes, culture and cuisine all mixed together with love and care, laughs and memories.

Starting with my Mauritian grandma's cookbook who was my first inspiration, which is still somewhere in the attic, I've always had a passion for discovering new recipes and casually documenting them. Many moons ago, my own sister Caroline gave me the idea of a cookbook of my own when she said to me, "If you write a cookbook, I'll be the first to buy a copy!"

All praise is due to the Creator, I converted to Islam ten years ago via Christianity and pan-Africanism. I am also blessed to have had an English mum and a South African father, and came from a foodie family that cooked dishes from many places. My English grandma, a creative cook, was great at making Christmas cake and steamed puddings, and my grandfather was a cook in the Royal Air Force during World War Two, as his flat feet made unfit to fight on the frontline. My Mauritian grandma was the best cook in my world, and we loved going to her house because of the delicious and spicy Creole food that she made.

Later on in life when I worked as a model and a makeup artist, I got to travel and taste wonderful foods from around the world. I've eaten Chinese-style frog's legs in Chelsea, swordfish from the blue lagoons of Jamaica, lamb's testicles with Bedouins in Tunisia, and blooming tea, served with a green tea dry flower, in the Egyptian Spice Market of Istanbul. Needless to say there is nothing in this cookbook for the more squeamish!

My passion for food has influenced how I create my own dishes. This book has many of my signature recipes for warmer weather, although there are a few soups suitable for colder climates that have been added in for good measure. Many Middle Eastern salads and starters have been influenced by the great Ottoman Empire, dishes such as *bamiya*, or ladies fingers, and tabouleh, a herby, bulgur wheat salad. There are Moroccan marinades, West African jollof rice, Caribbean goat curry, Indian dishes like biryani, Persian chicken in walnut and pomegranate sauce, and Salad Olivier, which has now become part of Spanish tapas. There are also healthy fruit smoothies that can be drunk at any time, as well as some naughty and tantalising puddings such as Lemon Polenta Cake.

Twenty years on when I reminded Caroline about what she had said to years ago and that I was now doing a cookbook, she said, "And I will still be the first one to buy it today!" So may Allah bless my family and my friends for all their support, their respect of my faith, and their support of my cooking. May Allah show the light of this beautiful religion that we know and love as Islam to everyone, amen! I have tears in my eyes as I write this, for I have found my spiritual home. Finally, all praise is due to Allah, Lord of the all the worlds, and all good in this book is from Allah and any error or mistake is from me, so please forgive me for that.

In peace,
Karimah bint Dawood

London
July 2011

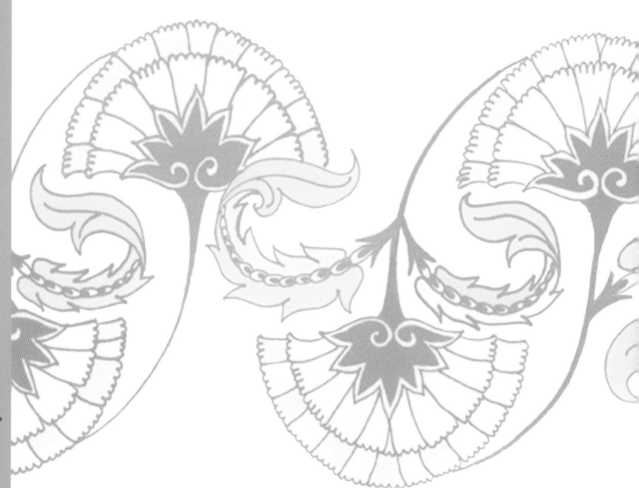

Soups

Bengali **Dhal Soup**

Serves 4

This is the sort of soup most of us have eaten when we go out for a curry, except that it's a little bit more authentic. Since embracing Islam, the Bengali community are my second adopted family after the Moroccan community, I even went on umrah with them. "Sis-stars" I know invite me to their homes, we pray and eat together and within these families I have been blessed to eat real Bengali food cooked by the loving hands of the women in the house.

Dhal soup is a nourishing, cheap, quick soup that's a great starter, low in calories but very tasty. Made of lentils, it's high in fibre and minerals like manganese which helps to reduce tiredness. This is a great soup for starting or breaking the fast in Ramadan, one of the pillars of Islam.

Preparation

1 Put the water in a saucepan. Then add the lentils, turmeric, bay leaf, peppercorns, lentils and salt (and optionally, the ginger and the chilli) to the pan and stir in with a wooden spoon. Bring the mixture to a boil, using a medium heat, while stirring. Then turn the heat down and simmer for about 15 or 20 minutes until the lentils are cooked. Keep stirring every five minutes to break up the lentils and to stop the soup from sticking to the bottom of the saucepan. They should be soft when crushed between the fingers, and most of the water should have boiled away.

2 Then add another 1 litre/35oz/3-5 cups of water depending how thick or thin you want the soup to be. Continue cooking on a medium to low heat and simmer for a further 10 to 15 minutes. Then turn off the heat and cover the saucepan with the lid.

3 Then put the ghee into a small frying pan, and heat to a medium temperature. Add the chopped onion and fry until the onions are clear, transparent and golden in colour. Then add the garlic and turn up the heat to medium-high and stir until the garlic and the onions are nearly brown. Be careful as garlic and onion burn easily. Take the frying pan off the heated ring, as it will still cook the garlic even when switched off. Stir in the sizzling onions and garlic to the soup, and then serve in bowls or mugs.

4 Squeeze fresh lemon juice into a jug and add an equal amount of olive oil to use as a dressing for the soup by adding 1-2 tablespoons and enjoy!

Ingredients

- 175g/6oz/1 cup red lentils (washed but not soaked)
- 720 ml/8oz/3 cups of cold water
- 5ml/1 tsp turmeric
- 5-10 crushed peppercorns, green or black
- 5ml/1 tsp salt
- 5ml/1 tsp minced fresh or powdered ginger (optional)
- 2½-5ml/½-1 tsp chilli powder (optional)
- 1 bay leaf
- 1 tbsp/15ml ghee (clarified butter)
- 1 small onion, chopped
- 1-3 cloves of garlic, chopped
- 15ml/2 tbsp lemon juice
- 30ml/2 tbsp olive oil

Did you know?

Turmeric, also known as curcumin, is a great anti-inflammatory for the joints and helps with stomach problems. Among Kashmiris, a teaspoon of turmeric, honey and hot milk is a great and effective bedtime drink for a tickly phlegmatic cough.

Faith **Chicken Soup**

Serves 4-6

This is a two-in-one recipe or I should say two meals out of one chicken. It's a variation on something a sister called Eman, a convert friend of mine, makes. As part of my faith as a Muslim, I believe it wrong to be wasteful, especially with food. Much to the dismay of my urbanite friends, I take this to the point of taking my food waste, like old tea bags, eggs shells, peelings, etc., to our local community garden. I think this is a good example so people can see that Muslims care about recycling and the environment. This has enabled me to make some great contacts with some lovely people who care about Allah's creation.

The recipe, a lovely, subtle soup is made from chicken stock and a succulent roast chicken, infused inside and out with exotic fragrant spices.

Preparation

1. Soak and wash the chicken in salt and lemon water, and then rinse and drain it. Leave it for 5 minutes to drain properly.

2. Put a litre of water into a large pot. Dissolve a stock cube in some boiling water and add to the pot. Place the whole chicken in the pot. Add the 2 chopped onions and 2 cloves of garlic to the pot and turn on the heat and bring to boil then turn down to simmer. Then add the cumin, turmeric, ginger, cinnamon, a bay leaf, pepper, salt and a pinch of saffron, and mix them into the broth.

3. Cover the pot and allow 30 minutes for a small chicken and 45 to 60 minutes for a large chicken. The chicken needs to be poached. It should not be cooked to the point where the flesh is falling off because you will need to get the chicken out in one piece in order to roast it. When the chicken is poached, the onions should have almost or completely dissolved. Remove the chicken using large metal forks and place it in a roasting dish to cool.

4. Then puree the coriander and parsley, the remaining onion and clove of garlic with the celery. This may have to be done in stages, depending on the size of your processor. You are looking to produce an herby paste that will go into the soup as stock.

5. Add the carrots and potatoes, diced into small or large pieces, whichever you prefer, and boil on a medium heat for 15 minutes. While the soup is boiling, prepare the okra and place it into the soup for the last 5 minutes. And voila! Your soup is ready: it's great as a starter or even as a breakfast treat!

Ingredients

- 1 chicken, small or large depending on how many you want to feed
- 1 litre/35oz/5 cups cold water
- 1 chicken/vegetable stock cube
- ½ bunch celery, coarsely chopped
- 3 small onions, finely chopped
- 3 cloves of garlic, finely chopped
- handful fresh coriander, washed and coarsely chopped
- handful fresh flat leaf parsley, washed and coarsely chopped
- 3 black dried lemons (or in powdered form)
- 5ml/1 tsp ginger powder
- 5ml/1 tsp turmeric powder
- 5ml/1 tsp ground pepper
- 5ml/1 tsp ground cinnamon
- 5ml/1 tsp ground black seeds
- salt (to taste)
- 3 medium carrots, peeled and diced small or large
- 2 medium potatoes, peeled and diced small or large
- 175g/½ oz/1 cup okra, topped and tailed
- 5ml/1 tsp cumin
- 1 bay leaf
- pinch saffron

Moroccan **Harira Soup**

Serves 8

Harira is eaten morning and night in Morocco and, during Ramadan, the custom is to break the fast by eating *harira* after having dates and milk; this soup is akin to the Pakistani *haleem* but without the wheat and is a meal in itself. As a convert to Islam, this soup is part of my early memories of being a Muslim. Shopping in Little Morocco in North Kensington in London, the greengrocers used to insist that I share their *harira* and *shebakia*, the sweet and nutty Moroccan cakes, to break the fast with them during Ramadan.

There are regional variations on *harira*: some people add corn flour to thicken it but it's not necessary as the red lentils thicken the soup enough anyway. Other people use baked garlic but during Ramadan I prefer not to. There is no one fixed *harira* recipe so please add your own variations, if Allah wills. To the horror of my traditional Moroccan friends, I add fresh okra to it to give it that healthy Karimah touch!

Preparation

1 Fry the onions and the celery in the olive oil until golden and then add the lamb and then brown it on a medium to high heat without burning it. Then turn the heat down to medium, and add the salt, pepper, basil, turmeric, cinnamon, and then stir them in gently. Then add the coriander and parsley and stir for another minute. Then add the washed and drained lentils, and you should see a beautiful mixture of colours in your pot. Lastly, add the tomatoes and the water and leave it to simmer for at least one hour on a low heat, stirring it occasionally and adding more water should the soup become too thick: remember it's a soup rather than a stew or curry.

2 When the soup is ready to serve, add the chickpeas and noodles and cook for a further 5 minutes adding at least another cup of water to rehydrate the noodles. Then turn the heat back up to medium and stir in the lemony eggs with a long wooden spoon. Continue stirring slowly in order to create long egg strands and to thicken the soup.

3 Season with the finely chopped mint leaves and serve in bowls. Put a teaspoon of ground cinnamon into a tea strainer and shake a little of the cinnamon gently into each bowl of soup, distributing the cinnamon equally between each bowl. Serve with a lemon and olive dressing and don't forget to pray for me and others in your prayers when you break your fast with this soup!

Ingredients

- 500g/1 lb lamb, diced into small cubes
- 15ml/1 tbsp olive oil, for frying
- 5ml/1 tsp turmeric
- 5ml/1 tsp ground pepper
- 5ml/1 tsp ground cinnamon
- 5ml/1 tsp dried basil
- 5ml/1 tsp salt
- 25ml/1oz/1 cup celery and celery leaves, chopped
- 3 small onions, chopped
- 20ml/¾oz/1 cup parsley, chopped
- 20ml/¾oz/1 cup coriander, chopped
- 10ml/½ cup fresh mint leaves, finely chopped
- 240g/8½oz/1 can of tomatoes, drained and chopped
- 5ml/1 tsp salt
- 150ml/4 fl oz/¾ cup red lentils
- 1 litre/2 pints/4¼ cups water
- 280g/9oz/1 tin chickpeas, drained
- 30g/3oz/1-2 cups vermicelli fine soup noodles
- 2 eggs, beaten with the juice of 1 lemon, prepared at the last minute

Did you know?

Okra has great medicinal qualities in soothing stomach complaints. It cleanses the body and helps in the elimination of toxins.

Queen **Efua's Soup**

Overeating and eating the wrong combination of foods is a common problem during Ramadan. This wonderful soup is a great rectifier of the digestive system, as Allah wills.

This laxative soup is inspired by the African-American naturopath Queen Efua, whose writing has been a source of enlightenment to me about the amazing health benefits of okra. Leeks have similar nutritional benefits as do onions and garlic. They provide a good source of fibre, folic acid, vitamins B6 and C, manganese and iron.

This recipe also contains an optional mild laxative called cascara sagrada, but it is *not* recommended for use by pregnant women or children under the age of 12, so it can easily be left out if needed.

Preparation

1 Prepare the okra and onion or leek and set aside. Add 1 dessert spoon of oil to a medium-size pot. Fry the cumin seeds and chilli on a medium heat. Then add the chopped leek or onion and fry until golden. Add turmeric and fry everything together for a minute. Then add the okra and fry everything together for 5 minutes. Then add the vegetable buillion stock and a pinch of sea salt. Bring to the boil and simmer for 5 minutes on a low medium heat.

2 This soup is a great starter and will do wonders for you digestive system and other ailments. Serve in soup bowls and enhance your life!

Ingredients

- 500g/1 lb/3 cups chopped okra, topped and tailed
- 30ml/1 cup parsley
- 1 leek or onion, chopped
- 10ml/2 tsp sunflower oil
- 500ml/2 cups vegetable buillion stock
- 5ml/1 tsp cascara sarada (optional)
- 5ml/1 tsp turmeric
- 5ml/1 tsp cumin seeds
- 5ml/1 tsp broken dried red chillies
- A pinch of sea salt

Did you know?

Okra has great medicinal qualities in soothing stomach complaints. It cleanses the body and helps in the elimination of toxins. It is low in calories yet is a good source of nutrients including Vitamin B6 and C, fibre, calcium, and folic acid. It is effective in the prevention of neural tube defects in developing foetuses mainly due to its high content of Vitamin B6, calcium, fibre, and folic acid.

Oriental
Butternut Squash Soup

Serves 4

Soups are comforting and squash, which is part of the pumpkin, melon, and cucumber family, was one of the favourite foods of the Prophet, peace be upon him, which he used to eat with dates. Squash relieves an inflamed stomach, is high in fibre so is good for the heart and is also high in potassium and Vitamin C. It is best complemented with ginger which aids the digestion and is good for the liver; it's also an aphrodisiac and should be eaten with caution by single persons who are in good health.

The lemon grass and coconut give this soup that exotic Oriental taste that would make a great starter for a main course like biryani, chicken satay, noodles and even African jollof rice. It's also very quick to make, taking only half an hour to make.

Preparation

1 Put the ghee or vegetable oil into a large saucepan on a medium heat and let it melt. Add the onions, garlic, ginger and lemon grass and fry them gently until golden yellow, but if your onions do get a bit brown, don't worry. Then add the squash, potatoes and the herbs and stir.

2 Put the stock cube and the coconut cream in a heat-proof jug and dissolve in three cups of boiling water, and add it to the mixture. Add another three cups of water so that everything is neatly covered. Turn up the heat and bring to boil for five minutes and then turn the heat down low. Cover the pot with a lid and simmer for another 15 minutes. Turn heat off and leave to cool before blending.

3 Put the cooled soup using a small cup or mug into a processor and blitz it for a few seconds until the soup has a smooth texture. Return to the pot, add salt and pepper, and reheat before serving. At the re-heating stage you can add some fresh top-and-tailed okra and cook for 15minutes in the soup. You could also fry some onions and green chilli in a separate frying pan and add on top of the soup before serving like the Bengali Dhal Soup. The possibilities are endless when there is soup to be eaten!

Ingredients

- 1 medium-sized butternut squash, peeled and diced
- 3 medium-sized potatoes, peeled and chopped into large pieces
- 3 small onions, finely chopped
- 3 cloves of garlic, crushed
- 1⅕"/3cm piece of fresh ginger, finely chopped
- 1 fresh lemon grass stick, peeled and chopped
- 1 cup of celery, coriander and parsley, chopped
- 15ml/1 tbsp butter, ghee or vegetable oil
- 1 vegetable stock cube
- 25g/1 oz coconut cream
- 3pt/1½l/6 cups of boiling water
- 5ml/1 tsp sea salt
- 15ml/3 tsp black pepper
- 50g/2 oz/½ cup okra (optional)

Did you know?

"The Holy Prophet, peace be upon him, amongst all other foods, liked pumpkin." (Tirmidhi)

Salads

Beetroot Salad

Serves 4-6

There are many versions of beetroot salad or salsa. As a young child, I ate beetroot, onions and vinegar with my Asian grandma, and this got passed down to my English mum and now we are trying an old Ottoman version of the same recipe. Beetroot is an extremely important vegetable that is often overlooked: it s good for heart problems, cholesterol and is considered by some doctors as a super-food as it has an amazing effect on lowering blood pressure.

Preparation

1 Boil the beetroots in salted water until tender, for one to two hours depending on their size. You will know they are tender when they can be easily pierced with a skewer. Drain them and leave to cool in cold water. When cool remove their skins, although you will get pink fingers! Just think that if you'd done henna the day before you might come up with some gorgeous new look!

2 Meanwhile make the dressing by whisking all the other ingredients together, except the yoghurt, in a bowl. Cut the beetroot into 1-2 cm cubes and mix with the prepared vinaigrette. Place in a lidded container and chill in the fridge before serving. Serve alone or spooned with some yoghurt sprinkled with ground cumin on the plate, or as a layer in the Moroccan Salad Tower. The Lebanese add tahini to the yogurt and the Turkish add garlic: the world's your oyster with Muslim cuisines as there is so much to choose from, praise Allah.

Ingredients

- 400g/1 lb/4-5 fresh unpeeled beetroots, washed and left whole
- 45ml/3 tbsp olive oil
- 30ml/2 tbsp apple cider vinegar
- zest of half a large orange
- 45ml/3 tbsp freshly squeezed orange juice
- 3ml/½ tsp cinnamon
- 3ml/½ tsp cayenne pepper
- 15ml/3 tsp chopped mint
- salt and pepper to taste
- whole plain yoghurt to serve (optional)

Maghrebi
Orange and **Carrot Salad**

Serves 4-6

This unusual North African orange and carrot salad, commonly made in the Maghreb, is fresh, sweet and juicy, and it quenches the thirst on many levels, being full of vitamins and minerals and bursting with vibrant energy.

Preparation

On a plate, slice the orange across the fruit to get circular slices, and save three slices for decoration and chop the remaining slices into quarters, being careful to retain any juice that comes out. Mix the orange juice with sugar, lemon juice, orange flower water, cinnamon and salt to taste to make the dressing. Stir the dressing into the carrots, oranges and chill in the fridge. Depending on how much juice there is, you may want to drain some off before serving or you may want to use any excess as part of the Moroccan Salad Tower, so retain the juice and decorate with orange slices, and garnish with freshly chopped coriander.

Ingredients

* 500gms/1 lb. carrots, peeled and grated
* 1 large orange, peeled
* 5ml/1 tsp cinnamon
* 5ml/1 tsp brown sugar
* 45ml/3 tbsp lemon juice
* 15ml/1 tbsp orange flower water
* Salt to taste

Lemon and Sumac Couscous Salad

Serves 4-6

Couscous is a great comfort food when eaten hot but it is also a delicious snack when eaten cold. It's a delicate little thing which is not to be left in the fridge for more than a couple of days if you are preparing it beforehand. Seasoned with an unusual Middle Eastern spice called *sumac* (which is also used as a treatment for stomach complaints and fever in Muslim countries), it adds a sour taste that compliments the lemon and mint.

Preparation

1 Place the couscous in a heatproof bowl and add hot water. Cover with a clean dry tea towel and allow the steam to cook the couscous. After ten minutes, put a fork through the couscous to loosen the grains.

2 Meanwhile roast the peppers on the gas hob or cut them in half lengthwise and grill both sides until their skins are blacked. Place them in a clean plastic bag until cool and then remove their skins, and then cut them into chunky slices. Grill circular slices of courgette or fry them in a teaspoon of oil until golden brown. Sprinkle sumac, salt and pepper over the couscous, and fork them through which lifts and separates the grains again. Grate the skin off a lemon over the bowl of couscous, add the roasted chopped vegetables and dress with olive oil and lemon juice. Toss everything together until well mixed. Sprinkle with mint and serve as snack, side salad or as part of the Moroccan Salad Tower.

Ingredients

- 470g/25oz/2 cups of dry couscous, white or brown
- 470g/25oz/2 cups boiling water
- 1 green bell pepper
- 1 yellow bell pepper
- 2 medium-sized courgettes/ zucchini
- 5 spring onions
- 15ml/1 tbsp sumac
- 3ml/½ tsp sea salt
- 5ml /1 tsp black pepper
- 15ml/1 tbsp olive oil
- 15ml/1 tbsp lemon juice
- zest of 1 lemon
- 30ml/1oz/¼ cup fresh mint leaves, chopped

Mediterranean
Green Salad

Serves 4-6

A fresh green salad with sun-kissed olives and tomatoes.

Preparation

1 Wash and drain the lettuce, cucumber and tomatoes. Peel the onion and then finely chop it, either into slices or small pieces as you prefer. Chop the lettuce into strips about one centimetre wide and five centimetres in length; the leaves can be layered to do this more quickly. And cut the tomatoes into the same sized strips as the lettuce. Cut the cucumber in half lengthways, then lay the flat side of each half on to the cutting board and make more slices down the length of the cucumber. Hold them together with your fingers and cut across in ½-1 centimetre slices

2 Wash and dry the coriander and parsley and chop finely. Put the salt and pepper in a cup and add the juice of one lemon with the olive oil. Mix all the salad vegetables and herbs together in a bowl and pour the dressing over, adding olives as a garnish. Voila! And here is a Mediterranean salad to bring a fresh burst of sunshine to your plate!

Ingredients

- 1 iceberg lettuce or Cos lettuce or 2 little gem lettuces
- 3 large tomatoes
- ½ cucumber
- 1 medium onion, sliced or chopped
- 75ml/3oz/½ cup green or black pitted olives
- 100g/3oz/½ cup fresh coriander and parsley, finely chopped
- 1 lemon
- 85ml/2oz/¼ cup virgin olive oil
- 5ml/1 tsp black pepper
- 2½ml/½ tsp sea salt

Rice Salad

Serves 4-6

This interesting and zingy rice salad is perfect for refreshing those summer taste buds as a starter, or as a side dish or as one of those base layers of a Moroccan Salad Tower.

Preparation

1 Wash and cook the basmati rice and the mixed vegetables together, allowing 12 minutes for white basmati, and 20 minutes for brown basmati. Drain when cooked and rinse with cold water so that the grains do not stick together, and then set aside to drain.

2 You should be quick with this next stage as when rice cools it quickly produces bacteria. In a medium bowl, whisk together the yogurt, oil, and curry powder. Stir in the rice, apples, green onions, raisins and chives and mix well. Season to taste with salt and pepper. Place in a lidded container and chill in the fridge for at least 20 minutes.

Ingredients

- 470ml/2 cups basmati rice200ml/1 cup frozen mixed veg
- 235ml/1 cup low fat plain yoghurt15ml/1 tbsp olive oil15ml/1 tbsp curry powder, to taste30ml/2 tbsp apple cider vinegar
- 1 green apple, peeled and chopped
- 150ml/2½ oz/½ cup green onions, chopped30ml/2 tbsp golden raisins 30ml/2 tbsp fresh chives, snipped salt and black pepper to taste

Rainbow Salad

Serves 4-6

This fresh creamy vegetable salad takes me back to my Rasta days, when I was inspired by a naturopath called Queen Efua. I have been making this salad for years: it's a take on conventional coleslaw, full of essential minerals and vitamins. For an extra healthy option, use light mayonnaise or even soya mayonnaise which is available from health food shops. If you suffer from high blood pressure, one tablespoon of soya salt is enough as its salt content is high.

Preparation

Wash all the vegetables and grate either by hand or in a food processor. Mix the soya sauce and mayonnaise in a jug, and, at this point, you can add additional seasoning like ginger, garlic or lemon grass, if you like. Pour the dressing over the vegetables and gently stir together Garnish and decorate with washed and finely chopped parsley and enjoy!

Ingredients

- ½ white cabbage, grated
- ½ red cabbage, grated
- 3 carrots, grated
- 1 beetroot, peeled and grated
- 45-75ml/3-5 tbsp mayonnaise
- 45ml/3 tbsp dark soya sauce
- 5ml/1 tsp pepper
- handful of parsley, chopped

Salad Olivier

Serves 8-10

I discovered this famous Iranian salad when I was at college with some fellow Iranian students, and loved it and had to find out how it was made. This salad is also part of Spanish tapas – so it must have made its way along the Silk Route and found its way into Spanish cuisine! This particular version is thought to have been invented in Moscow in 1860 by a Russian chef called Lucien Olivier, who cooked at a restaurant called the Hermitage. It was revolutionary at the time but in today's culinary climate it is basically a glorified potato salad. Once you get the hang of it you can experiment and try out different vegetables and meats, and maybe even fish and seafood, but this salad must always contain dill and pickled gherkins. But don't add too much spice or it will turn into something that tastes like coronation chicken.

Preparation

1 Soak the chicken in a large bowl or sink with three tablespoons of salt and the juice of one lemon; let this soak for at least 15 minutes as this will clean any grime off the bird. Rinse the chicken inside and out and set aside in a sieve or colander for 15 minutes to drain.

2 Place the chicken in saucepan large enough to contain it and the eggs. Put enough cold water into the saucepan so that chicken and eggs are covered. Add two tablespoons of fresh dill (for dry, use one teaspoon), and the chopped onion. Bring it to the boil, and then turn to heat down and leave to simmer for 40 minutes. Potatoes can be placed on top in a steamer, which saves time and energy, or boil them separately for 20 minutes. In a separate small saucepan cook the frozen mixed vegetables in boiling water for 5 minutes, drain and leave to cool.

3 Once done, leave the chicken to cool down, and, when cool enough, take the eggs out and put them in cold water, as well as letting the potatoes cool down too. Take the chicken out of the stock and leave it on a plate to cool. When cool, peel of the chicken skin and then take all the flesh off the bones.

4 Combine the cooked chicken pieces, mashed potatoes, carrots, peas, chopped onion and dill pickle, hard-boiled eggs and capers. Fold slightly to mix, and then, use a knife to break it all up. Mix the mayonnaise, sour cream, mustard, lemon juice, pepper, salt and black pepper and three tablespoons of fresh dill (or one teaspoon of dried dill) to make the dressing. Pour over the salad and mix thoroughly and gently. Cover the bowl and chill well in the fridge. To serve, put the salad upon a bed of lettuce leaves on a large platter. Garnish with black olive slices, sliced hard-boiled egg, tomato wedges and parsley sprigs, and sprinkle with a little paprika.

Ingredients

- 1 whole baby chicken, skin left on
- 500g/1¼ lb potatoes
- 1-3 large sour dill gherkins, chopped finely
- 235ml/1 cup frozen mixed vegetables, cooked
- 2 hard-boiled eggs, peeled and coarsely chopped
- 1 hard-boiled egg, sliced, for decoration
- 30ml/2 tbsp of capers, drained
- 235ml/1 cup mayonnaise
- 15ml/1 tbsp Dijon mustard
- 10ml/2 tsp fresh lemon juice
- 5ml/1 tsp salt
- 10ml/2 tsp black pepper, crushed
- 1 onion, chopped
- 25ml/5 tbsp of fresh dill, washed and finely chopped
- 10-20 black or green olives, halved for decoration
- parsley sprigs
- 1 large ripe tomato, cut into small wedges
- lettuce leaves, washed and dried
- pinch paprika

Did you know?

Dill has many health benefits. It promotes the digestion, stimulates the appetite and is good for ameliorating insomnia, hiccups, diarrhoea, dysentery, menstrual disorders, respiratory disorders and oral care.

Salsa de Cebolla
(Tomato and Onion Relish)

Serves 4

This cool, slightly sweet summer salsa will have you shimmying round the table: its fresh zingy flavours will bring your taste-buds back to life, Allah willing. It can be used as a dip, a marinade for vegetables like asparagus, an accompaniment for barbecued meats or to top toasted bread. While researching this recipe, I realized that South Africans make a variant using instead carrot and onion or cucumber and onion; it's amazing that dishes like this are so cross cultural! Salsa fresh flavours are like summer chutney, and salsa is an accompaniment rather than a dish in itself.

Preparation

Prepare the red onion, tomatoes and mint leaves; a food processor cuts out the tears in preparing the onions. Place them in a bowl, and add the sea salt and black pepper. Then add vinegar and mix, adding additional vinegar if needed. Allow to marinate for an hour before serving, or refrigerate if the salsa is not being served immediately. It may be stored in the fridge for up to three days. It can also be served with tapas, mezze or a tali.

Ingredients

- 1 medium red onion, thinly sliced or chopped
- 2 firm tomatoes, thinly sliced or chopped
- 60ml/4 tbsp/¼ cup sherry vinegar/balsamic vinegar/apple cider vinegar
- 5 fresh mint leaves, finely chopped
- sea salt and black pepper, to taste

Luxury **Potato Salad**

Serves 8-10

Preparation

1 Lightly roast the walnuts, place in a hot oven (about 200C/400F/Gas 6) or do them on the grill for a few minutes until they begin to colour slightly. This gives the walnuts a fresher, less bitter taste. Put the vinegar, mustard seeds, oils, honey, salt and pepper in a screw-top jar or in the bowl of a small hand blender. Shake or blend until creamy. And then add more seasoning to taste if necessary.

2 Boil the potatoes, and I prefer Jersey Royals or Charlotte potatoes, in salted water or preferably steam them for about 15-20 minutes until just tender but still firm. Drain well and, then, when cool enough to handle, cut them into small pieces about 2cm or 1 inch square at the most. Place the potatoes in a mixing bowl with the tarragon, shallots, gherkins and walnuts, and pour in the dressing. Serve warm or, if you're not eating straight away, refrigerate in a lidded container but leave out to return the salad to room temperature before eating.

Ingredients

- 900g/2 lb new potatoes, washed or scrubbed
- 50ml/2 tbsp walnut pieces (optional)
- 15ml/1 tbsp tarragon vinegar or apple cider vinegar
- 30ml/2 tsp black mustard seeds crushed
- 30ml/2 tbsp olive oil
- 15ml/1 tbsp walnut oil
- 45ml/3 tsp mayonnaise
- 5-10ml/1-2 tsp black pepper, coarsely ground
- pinch flaked sea salt
- 10ml/1 tbsp fresh tarragon, chopped
- 1 large onion, finely chopped
- 30ml/2 tbsp gherkins, chopped (optional)

Recipe Idea: Moroccan Salad Tower

This starter would do most people as a main course as it's so filling. In the Arab world generally, salads are an important part of any meal. These salads are layered – Beetroot Salad, Maghrebi Orange and Carrot Salad, Lemon and Sumac Couscous Salad, and Luxury Potato Salad – one on top of the other so that everybody gets something of everything. This meal consists of layering these salads as follows, then dressing them with prawns and seafood dressing and avocados. At the same time, all these salads could be served separately.

Shaken **Aubergine Salad**

Serves 4-6

This salad forms part of the mezze of Middle Eastern Mediterranean starters, which is taken from an old Ottoman recipe but with a twist of my own. When I first saw aubergines cooking on the gas hob I was amazed that they cooked so quickly and thoroughly.

Preparation

1 Wash and dry the aubergines, peppers and chillies. Using a gas hob cook each vegetable individually until their skins are charred black all over. When cooked, seal them in a freezer bag leave to cool. If you don't have a gas cooker, bake them in medium heat until their skins are charred black (but watch out for the chillies as they take less time). Once cooled, remove their blackened skins, rinse and dry them on kitchen towels, cut them into chunky pieces and place in an airtight container. Then crush the garlic cloves, and mix with the lemon juice, olive oil, and salt and pepper. Dress the vegetables, gently stirring and shaking them, and then cover and refrigerate, allowing them to marinade in the dressing.

2 This dish can be made a few days before serving and can be served with mezze tapas, and even as an accompaniment to South Asian cooking. For anyone with arthritis, it's better not to eat too much of sweet peppers or aubergine.

Ingredients

- 2 large aubergines
- 3 red sweet peppers
- 3 red chillies or 5 green chillies
- 5 cloves of garlic
- 1 lemon juice
- 15ml/1 tbsp of olive oil
- salt
- pepper

Tabouleh Salad

Serves 4-6

Tabouleh is a green salad that is quick and easy to make, especially with a food processor. Many years prior to being Muslim, I always seemed to have Muslim friends, who were always generous and hospitable, and used to invite me and a friend to eat with them. I remember first experiencing the mezze of Lebanese cuisine on one such occasion at an expensive restaurant overlooking Green Park in central London. Tabouleh salad is part of mezze and it acts as a citric refresher for the palate in contrast with all the nutty and meaty flavours you find in mezze dishes. It is traditionally made with parsley but I also add coriander, as both herbs are high in nutritional properties and are good for mind and body. It was the respect and generosity of these people that attracted me to Islam and as I learnt more about the character of the Prophet, peace be upon him, I realized that generosity is a big part of Muslim life.

Preparation

Cover the bulgur wheat with hot water 1-2 inches or 2½-5 centimetres higher than the level of the wheat and leave to soak for at least 30 minutes. Squeeze out excess water out of the bulgur wheat using a large square of muslin or a clean tea towel. Combine with all the finely chopped parsley, coriander and mint. Line the serving bowl with grape leaves or romaine lettuce, and lay the mixture on top. Mix together the olive oil, lemon juice, salt and pepper and then dress the salad. It can be served immediately or chilled.

Ingredients

- 1 bunch fresh parsley, chopped
- 1 bunch of fresh coriander, chopped
- 30ml/2 tbsp fresh mint, chopped
- 1 medium onion, finely chopped
- 5 medium tomatoes, diced
- 5ml/1 tsp salt
- 5ml/1 tsp black pepper
- 120ml/½ cup bulgur wheat
- 75ml/5 tbsp lemon juice
- 75ml/5 tbsp extra virgin olive oil

Asian Greens

Serves 4-6

Before I became Muslim, I used to hate greens at school or home that were boiled to death and had no flavour, but after becoming Muslim – hey presto – I discovered Asian greens, which are fragrant and tickle your taste buds and you can get all those wonderful, essential vitamins inside you!

Preparation

Heat the oil in a large non-stick wok or karahi pan, and sizzle the cumin and mustard seeds for one minute, then add the chilli, ginger and turmeric. Fry until the fragrance of the spices can be smelt, usually for a couple of minutes. Then add the greens a bit at a time, tossing them in the spices, gradually adding more; this way the spices get infused into the greens. Add the salt and water, and cover the pan and cook for 4-5 minutes until the greens have softened. Finally, add the lemon juice, and half the desiccated coconut, and then toss everything together. Put into a serving dish and garnish with the rest of the coconut.

Ingredients

- 15ml/1 tbsp vegetable oil
- 10ml/2 tsp cumin seeds
- 5ml/1 tsp mustard seeds
- 1-7 green chillies, finely chopped (optional)
- fresh root ginger, grated (optional)
- 5-15ml/1-3 tsp turmeric
- 500g/1 lb 1½ oz shredded greens
- juice of 1 lemon
- 30ml/2 tbsp unsweetened desiccated coconut
- 120ml/4 fl oz/½ cup water
- a pinch of salt

Pakistani Fruit Salad

Serves 4-6

Eating fruit on an empty stomach has great health benefits, and, in researching the different ways various cultures break the fast, I came upon this Pakistani fruit salad recipe, which is a bit of an acquired taste: the salty *chat masala* mix can be bought in any Indian food store.

Preparation

Wash the apples, grapes, and peaches, peel the oranges, bananas, apples and peaches, and cut all the fruit into chunks, removing the stones where necessary. Peel and slice the guava fruit and add to the other fruits in a bowl. Mix them together carefully with a dressing of lemon juice, sugar, salt, and *chat masala*, and then chill in the refrigerator for two hours.

Ingredients

- 2 apples
- 2 oranges
- 1 handful of grapes
- 4 peaches
- 4 guava fruit
- 3 bananas
- 60ml/4 tbsp sugar
- 30ml/2 tbsp lemon juice
- 5ml/1 tsp chat masala spice mix

Snacks

Lebanese **Humous**

Serves 2-4

This vegetarian starter snack is quick and easy to make and more flavoursome than anything you can buy in the shops. Prior to Islam, I used to be a Rasta like Bob Marley and had dreadlocks, which I usually kept covered in a scarf. I was vegetarian for a long time and ate lots of humous. I was told at the time that tahini, a sesame paste, has lots of Vitamin B which helps to repel mosquitoes, and explains why so much Middle Eastern food contains sesame seeds.

Preparation

1 Drain and rinse the canned chickpeas and put them into a food processor with the lemon juice, garlic, cumin, salt, tahini, and water, and blend it until creamy in texture. If it's still too thick then add more lemon juice, and, if necessary, garlic, cumin or salt to taste. Using a spatula, scrape the humous out into a bowl or a plate, making it smooth with the back of a spoon. Drizzle with some extra virgin olive oil and garnish with the coriander; alternatively, you can sprinkle some paprika on it.

2 Humous is an amazingly versatile spread, which can be served with bread, pitta, naan, or garlic bread. It's also a dipping sauce for tapas, meatballs and crudités, such as celery and carrot sticks, spring onions, and fresh tomatoes. It can even be thinned down further with water and lemon juice and used as a salad dressing.

Ingredients

- 200g/7oz canned chickpeas
- 30ml/2 tbsp lemon juice or more
- 3 garlic cloves, crushed
- 5ml/1 tsp ground cumin
- pinch salt
- 60ml/4 tbsp tahini
- 60ml/4 tbsp water
- 30ml/2 tbsp extra virgin olive oil
- 5ml/1 tsp paprika
- coriander leaves, freshly chopped, for garnish

Karimah's
Salt Fish Fritters

Makes 15-20 fritters

These tasty fritters are so delicious I just had to include them, as they are part of my memories of my Rasta days. You can season them according to you own taste. They can be served alone, with salad or as part of tapas or mezze. They are not ideal when you are fasting because they are so salty.

Preparation

1 Soak the codfish in water overnight to remove excess salt, and the boil in fresh water on a medium heat for 30 minutes to remove more salt. Drain, leave to cool, and break the salt fish with your fingers to take out any bones. Dice, shred finely, and set aside. Fry the onions, spring onions, garlic, peppers and the salt and pepper, and fry in a skillet using a small amount of oil, then set aside in a bowl once it's ready.

2 While the cooked fish and the fried onions are cooling down, place the flour and the dried seasoning in a large bowl, and then add the fish and onion mixture to the flour and then slowly add the cup of water creating a dough-like batter. Put a centimetre of oil in a heavy frying pan on a medium heat. Spoon the batter in the pan using a large spoon, turning over to do five minutes on each side, frying until golden brown and crisp on both sides. Drain on paper towels and keep in a dish in a warm oven until ready to serve.

Ingredients

- 350g/12oz salted codfish (boneless where possible)
- 350g/12oz/1½ cup flour
- 120ml/3 oz/¾ cup water
- 3 medium-sized onions
- 6 stalks spring onions, chopped (optional)
- 25ml/2 tbsp vegetable oil
- 180ml/3 oz/1½ cup fresh coriander, finely chopped
- 2-3 scotch bonnet peppers, finely chopped
- 3 cloves garlic
- 15ml/3 tsp paprika
- 5ml/1 tsp ground cumin
- 5ml/1 tsp ground coriander
- 5ml/1 tsp turmeric
- 15ml/3 tsp black pepper

Moroccan
Lemon Chicken Wings

When I first tried whole lemon chicken in the Moroccan style, I thought what a great marinade for barbequed chicken pieces. The lemon and ginger in the marinade perfectly compliment the chicken and give it that far away taste of Arabian Nights.

Preparation

1 Wash and drain the herbs; hanging them in bunches from kitchen hooks is very effective. Wash and soak the chicken for at least 15 minutes in lemon juice and salt water, then rinse and drain. Using a food processor, coarsely chop the herbs, peel the garlic and place all ingredients except the chicken pieces into the processor and blend into a coarse paste – this is your marinade. With clean hands, put half of the marinade into a lidded jar or container and place in the fridge for use on another day. Then rub the remaining half of the marinade over the chicken pieces in a bowl and leave in the fridge (or a cool place which is less than 10°C/50°F) for at least an hour. Grill, roast or barbeque the chicken pieces for around 30 minutes, remembering to turn them over after 15 minutes. Please note that barbequing is usually quicker than grilling or roasting. Serve as part of your tapas or mezze platter.

2 The remaining marinade can be smeared over the inside and out of a whole chicken and left to marinade in the same way, and then roasted, covered with foil or a lid for an hour and a half. You can put some olives inside the chicken 30 minutes from the end.

Ingredients

- 1 kilo/2 lbs/4 cups chicken wings or drumsticks
- 120g/4oz/2 cups fresh coriander
- 120g/4oz/2 cups flat leaf parsley
- 1 bulb garlic, peeled and crushed
- 125ml/4oz/½ cup Moroccan olive oil
- 1 tbsp coarse sea salt
- zest of 1 unwaxed lemon
- 60ml/2oz/4 tbsp lemon juice
- 5ml/1 tsp ground cumin
- 5ml/1tsp ground coriander
- 5ml/1 tsp ground ginger
- 5ml/1 tsp turmeric

Moorish **Kebabs**

Makes 20 kebabs

Since the Muslims lived and ruled Spain for about 800 years, Moorish cooking has heavily influenced its cuisine up until the present day. These juicy little meat burgers will leave you wanting "moor"!

Preparation

Combine all ingredients together with your hands in a bowl and then cover it and leave to marinade in fridge for at least an hour. Divide into small balls the size of golf balls and fry in shallow oil on a medium heat, and keep turning them for 15-20 minutes till brown on all sides. Drain on a plate using absorbent kitchen towels to remove access oil, and serve in bowl along with other tapas dishes. These kebabs are great finger food!

Ingredients

- 450g/1 lb minced beef or lamb or a combination
- 1 medium onion, finely chopped
- 2 tsp paprika
- 10ml/2 tsp cumin
- 5ml/1 tsp sea salt
- 5ml/1 tsp black pepper
- ½ tsp/2½ml hot ground chilli
- 45ml/3 tbsp Moroccan marinade
- 2½ml/½ tsp cinnamon (optional)
- 15ml/1 tbsp mint/oregano leaves (optional)

Lebanese **Kibbeh**

Makes 20 Kibbeh

Kibbeh is one of those foods that you crave, which isn't satisfied until you eat it. They are Middle Eastern meatballs filled with a softly-spiced pine nut filling. There are many recipes for kibbeh, but this one is perfect for beginners. Kibbeh form part of mezze, and are ideal as snacks or for picnics.

Preparation

1 Soak the bulgur wheat for 30 minutes in cold water and then drain. Remove any excess water by squeezing the bulgur wheat in a cheesecloth. Place into medium bowl and combine with half of the meat, the coarsely chopped onion, one teaspoon of salt and one teaspoon of pepper, and an egg. Combine well and place in small amounts in a food processor until it has a dough-like consistency. You can add an ice cube while processing to keep the mixture cool if necessary. Place the mixture aside and cover. Using a food processor is preferable, as using a mortar and pestle will take over an hour to achieve the desired consistency.

2 To prepare the kibbeh stuffing, sauté the finely chopped onion in olive oil in a medium-sized frying pan, and then add the pine nuts, if you are using them. Add the remaining half of the ground meat, making sure that it is properly divided up using a spatula. Then add the allspice, the cumin, and half a teaspoon each of salt and pepper. Once the meat is lightly browned, remove from the heat and allow to cool for 10 minutes.

3 To assemble the kibbeh, take an egg-sized amount of the shell mixture and form into a ball. With your finger, poke a hole in the ball, making a space for filling. Add the filling and pinch the top to seal the ball. You can then shape it as a ball or with a point. Then roll it in sesame seeds. Use a karahi or wok on a medium heat, using vegetable oil, for 10 minutes, until the sesame seeds turn golden brown. Use a slatted metal spoon to lower the meatball into the oil. It is best to do one kibbeh as a tester to see how hot the oil is. Uncooked kibbeh can be stored in the freezer in an airtight container for up to 3 months; they can easily be defrosted and fried.

Ingredients

- 900g/2 lbs/8 cups finely ground lean beef or lamb
- 45g/½ lb/2 cups bulgur cracked wheat
- 7½ml/1½ tsp salt
- 7½ml/1½ tsp pepper
- 1 egg
- 5ml/1 tsp allspice mix
- 2½ml/½ tsp cumin
- 1 medium onion, finely chopped
- 1 medium onion, coarsely chopped
- 90g/ 6oz/½ cup toasted pine nuts
- 15ml/1 tbsp olive oil
- sesame seeds
- sunflower oil, for deep frying

Did you know?

Pine nuts are rich in magnesium which help to alleviate muscle cramps, tension and fatigue, which are perfect for those who are fasting. Eating pine nuts on their own can react with some people, causing "pine mouth", which messes up your taste buds and leaves a metallic salty taste that can last anything between one to two weeks.

Lebanese **Mini-Pizza**

Serves 4-6

As a volunteer minibus driver for my local mosque, I sometimes take the over-55s sisters group strawberry picking and whenever we go out they spoil me with wonderful Middle Eastern food, praise Allah, including these scrumptious little pizzas. They can be made in advance and kept in foil in the fridge for a few days.

Preparation

1 Combine the filling ingredients in a bowl and leave aside. Just before you are ready to roll out dough, place on food processor and blitz for 20 seconds to get a smooth paste which is more Ottoman than rustic in inspiration! To make the dough, mix the yeast and sugar with the lukewarm water and leave for 15 minutes. Sift the flour and salt into a bowl, make a well in the centre, and add the oil and yeast mixture. Mix and knead to make a smooth and elastic dough, then cover and leave to rest for 30 minutes, or until it doubles in bulk. Once the dough is ready, divide the dough and keep dividing until you get equally-sized 20 pieces and then shape them into balls, otherwise you end up with too many or too few bases. Roll out each ball into a circle.

2 Spread 15ml or one tablespoon of the meat mixture on it. Arrange on an oiled oven tray, and bake in a pre-heated oven at Gas Mark 8/230°C/450°F for 10-15 minutes or until the crust is brown. These mini-pizzas can be served warm with the Ottoman Shaken Aubergine Salsa — they're scrumptious together.

Ingredients for the filling

- 200g/7oz/2 cups minced lamb
- 2 medium onions, chopped
- 5m/1 tsp baharat (Middle Eastern mixed spice)
- 2 large tomatoes, deseeded and finely chopped
- 5 sundried tomatoes
- 120g/4oz/½ cup pine nuts
- 30ml/2 tbsp sunflower oil
- 2½ ml/½ tsp salt
- 5ml/1 tsp black pepper

Ingredients for the base

- 15ml/1 tbsp dried yeast
- 15ml/1 tbsp sugar
- 235ml/4oz/1 cup lukewarm water
- 2.5 ml/½ tsp salt
- 330g/3 cups flour
- 60ml/4 tbsp sunflower oil

Pakoras

Makes 20 Pakoras

This tasty little high-protein snack reminds me of my vegetarian Rasta days when I used to get pakoras from Hindu sweet shops. Pakoras are vegetables in a chickpea flour batter known as gram flour, which is deep fried. Homemade ones are the best as the shop and restaurant-made ones tend to skimp on the veggies. Pakoras can be seasoned with fresh herbs and various combinations of spices, something as easy as Ethiopian barberry or just good old cumin and paprika. Pakoras make a great snack with yogurt and date chutney or as part of a mezze or tali. "O Mama, I'm licking my lips already!"

Preparation

1 Combine the flour, spices and salt in a bowl and mix together well. Add five tablespoons of cold water slowly, beating it until the mixture is smooth and free of lumps. Then add the grated vegetables and the chillies. Slowly add three tablespoons of water and continue to beat until well mixed. Check the consistency: it should resemble heavy cream and should easily coat a spoon. As courgettes are quite watery, you probably won't need any more water. Cover the batter and set aside for 10-15 minutes to let it settle.

2 Beat the batter again before frying and then, if you wish, add the baking powder to get a crispier crust. Fill a wok or karahi pan half way with sunflower oil and turn to a medium heat and leave to heat for five minutes. To check the oil is hot enough, take a teaspoon of the mixture and drop into the oil, it should sizzle! Drop a tablespoon of the pakora mix into the oil, and fry up to six at a time. Keep an eye on them, turning them with a slotted spoon until the pakoras are golden brown on all sides. Remove and drain on kitchen towels to drain off the excess oil. Serve immediately as part of a mezze or tali or just on their own!

Ingredients

- 310g/5oz/1⅓ cup chick pea flour, sifted
- 15ml/1 tbsp lemon juice
- 5ml/1 tsp green chillies, chopped
- 5ml/1 tsp turmeric
- 5ml/1 tsp garam masala
- 10ml/2 tsp ground coriander
- 5ml/1 tsp salt
- 9 tbsp cold water, as needed
- 5ml/1 level tsp baking powder (optional)
- 1 medium courgette, grated
- 1-3 medium carrots, grated
- sunflower oil for frying

Spanish **Tortilla** and **Potato Omelette**

Serves 4-6

Spain is where fun and excitement begins in terms of food. Travel south towards the equator and these presentations of tapas and mezze and talis hit the table. Being able to pick at little tastes of everything stimulate every area of my palate!

The Tortilla Espanola or Spanish Omelette is the most commonly-served dish in Spain. It is also called Tortilla de Patata or Potato Omelet. Bars and cafés serve it as a tapas or appetizer, but it is often served as a light dinner in Spanish homes. Because it is easy to transport, the Spanish make bocadillos or sandwiches by placing a piece between in a baguette. You can add other vegetables and herbs to tortilla like mushrooms, sweet corn, tomatoes, parsley, sweet corn and so on. As you get more confidence, just use your imagination.

Preparation

1 Cut the peeled potatoes into half lengthways. Then cut again into thin slices about ½cm/¼" or so, or into small cubes about 1-1½ cm/½" square. Peel and chop the onion into ½cm/¼" pieces.

2 Put potatoes into a bowl and season the mixture. While you could be typically Spanish and just use salt, there are plenty of alternatives: Italian basil and oregano, Asian spices, Moroccan paprika, cumin and coriander. It's up to you if you find salt alone a bit bland. Fry the potato pieces in the olive oil and when cooked take out and place in bowl. Alternatively you can steam the potato pieces for seven minutes until they are soft, and then leave them to cool.

3 Meanwhile crack and separate the eggs, using the shells to hold the yolk while you let the egg whites drain into a bowl. Whisk the egg whites until thick and fluffy and then add the yellow yolks, and stir gently together with a fork. Reuse the old olive oil and pour it into a small, non-stick frying pan (approximately 20-25cm/9-10") and put on a medium heat. Fry the onions until golden brown, and then add the potatoes into the pan and spread them out evenly. Then pour the egg mixture, stirring gently to make sure that it gets to bottom and all around the pan. Allow the egg to cook around the edges, then carefully lift up one side of the omelette to check if the egg has slightly "browned." The centre of the mixture should not be completely cooked and the egg should still be runny. When the mixture has browned on the bottom, you are ready to turn it over to cook the other side. Place a large dinner plate (30cm/12") upside down over the frying pan, and flip over quickly to let the omelette fall onto the plate.

4 Place the frying pan back on the cooker and put in just enough oil to cover the bottom and sides of the pan – approximately 7ml/1½ tsp. Let the pan warm for 30 seconds or so. Now slide the omelette into the frying pan, cooked side up, using a spatula to catch any egg mixture that runs out. Shape the sides of the omelette, and let it cook for 3-4 minutes. Turn the heat off and let the tortilla sit in the pan for five minutes. Carefully slide the omelette onto a plate and slice it into 6-8 pieces like a pie. It can be wrapped in tin foil and left to chill the fridge and can be served as part of your tapas meal.

Ingredients

- 6-7 medium potatoes, peeled
- 1 large yellow onion
- 5-6 large eggs
- 45ml/3 tbsp/⅙ cup olive oil
- Salt to taste

Smoothies

Caribbean
Carrot Juice Smoothie

Serves 4

As a rule Rastas are vegetarian or vegan, and when I was a Rasta before I became Muslim, I used to have all these wonderful and nutritious smoothies which are great with many of the different curries that Rastas make.

Preparation

Put grated carrots in a jug blender with a litre of water and blend for 30 seconds and leave in a large jug overnight in a cool place for the juice to mix in with the water. Strain out the grated carrot and, using muslin or a juicer, squeeze out any remaining juice and put it back into the jug. Discard the carrot pieces, ideally for composting. Empty the condensed milk into a separate large jug, and then, using a wooden spoon, stir in the spices or the essences, you don't have to have both. Pour in the carrot juice and stir well, until completely mixed and milky, and stir in the milk. Serve cold.

Ingredients

- 10 medium carrots, grated
- 1 litre/1¾ pints/8 cups filtered/bottled water
- 1 can/237ml/8 fl oz/1 cup condensed milk
- 2½ml/½ tsp vanilla essence (optional)
- 2½ml/½ tsp almond essence (optional)
- pinch nutmeg
- pinch cinnamon
- pinch green cardamom powder
- pinch ground cloves

Frozen Fruit Smoothie

Serves 2

When it's time to break the fast with dates and milk, all I want is juice, juice and more juice. As I feel so dehydrated, especially in the summer, this juice provides a natural fruit sugar high and lots of Vitamin C! You can freeze your own fruits after washing them or buy bags of frozen fruit from the supermarket. Kiwi fruit are a super food, good for your immune system and gives you a real boost when you are fasting. You can also use blackberries, blackcurrants, or mangoes, for this frozen smoothie or any other fruit you like in place of kiwi fruit.

Preparation

Wash, chop and freeze a punnet of strawberries and the kiwis for a minimum of three hours or alternatively use bought frozen fruits. Take the fruits out at least 15 minutes before you want to use them, otherwise there are like rocks in your blender. Put them into the blender with the apple juice and blend for 15 seconds or more until the ice breaks up. Serve in tall glasses with a sprig of mint, so cool and so very English.

Ingredients

- 450 g/16oz/3 cups strawberries, topped
- 3 kiwi fruit, peeled
- 235ml/8oz/1 cup apple juice
- sprig fresh mint (optional)

Peach Melba Smoothie

Serves 2

Here we go again, more variations on the smoothie vibe! This is a thick creamy smoothie that can be poured over ice.

Preparation

Wash all fruits and drain in a colander. Cut the stone out of the peaches and chop the flesh up. Blend the peaches and then add the raspberries, honey, apple juice and soya milk or yogurt and blend for 30 more seconds until smooth. Serve in a tall glass, and, if you prefer, over ice. Grate a little milk chocolate over the top for a heavenly touch!

Ingredients

- 235ml/8oz/1 cup apple juice
- 2 juicy peaches
- 450g/16oz/3cups/1 punnet raspberries
- 5ml/1 tsp honey
- 235ml/8oz/1 cup natural yogurt or soya milk

Mango Lassi

Serves 2-3

This delicious drink is the South Asian answer to milkshake; its natural sugars are a quick pick-me-up, accompanied with some lovely dates to break the fast with. Mango lassi is full of minerals, vitamins, antioxidants and fibre which adds the digestion and helps to keep your system clean. Lassi is usually yogurt-based and is mix with things like mint, salt, or rose-flower water; lassi drinks are a great accompaniment with hot spicy food and are very refreshing on a hot summer's day!

Preparation

Mango slices in tins are usually soft and pulpy, but fresh ripe mangoes are better. Put the yogurt, milk, water, mango, honey and pistachios in a blender and blitz it by pulsing it for 30 seconds; a handheld blender will do equally well. If you want to spice things up, add a little nutmeg or cinnamon or mixed spice, according to your preference, and pour the mix over ice in a glass and sip a taste of paradise, Allah willing!

Ingredients

- 765ml/12oz/3 cup plain yogurt
- 235 ml/4oz/1 cup milk
- 235ml/4oz/1 cup water
- 235ml/4oz/1 cup mango pulp/slices
- 5ml/1 tsp of honey
- 30ml/1oz pistachios, ground
- 2½ml/½ tsp cinnamon, mixed spice, or nutmeg to taste

Suhour Shake

Serves 2

This is a fast food way to start your day: it's a thick oat shake full of natural goodness. Get the blender out before you go to bed, wash the fruits and leave all the ingredients in the blender. all you have to do in the morning is switch the blender on. This shake is inspired by the Prophet's love of a particular kind of date, the 'Ajwa date, which, with a bit of effort, can be tracked down from specialist suppliers. It comes in the teachings of the Prophet, peace be upon him, that eating seven 'Ajwa dates each morning provides protection from poisons and magic for the day (Bukhari).

Preparation

Soak the dates in water overnight and remove them in the morning, this steeped water can be drunk separately while you blend the rest of the shake. Place all ingredients in a blender and pulse for 15 seconds, leave to rest and then pulse another 15 seconds. Pour into a large class, say bismillah ("In the name of God") and then drink.

Ingredients

- 480ml/8oz/2cup apple juice
- 1 banana, sliced
- 10ml/2 tsp honey
- 7 dates, soaked in water
- pinch cinnamon
- 200g/3oz/3/4 cup natural yogurt
- 30g/2 tbsp oats

Did you know?

Oats help to stabilize blood sugar and lower cholesterol levels; honey gives you energy and boosts immunity, and is full of anti-bacterial, anti-viral and anti-fungal agents; and cinnamon is an anti-inflammatory and helps to prevent blood clotting.

Ajwa Shake

Serves 1-2

This shake is also inspired by the Prophet's love of the 'Ajwa date, which, with a bit of effort, can be tracked down from specialist suppliers. This shake is a creative way to break your fast in a way that follows the Prophet's example.

Preparation

Take the stones out of the dates and put them in an empty glass jar with a lid and leave in the fridge to soak overnight or for a day. Take them out of the water and retain the water to drink separately, place the dates, milk and cinnamon or ginger in blender and blitz until smooth, pour in glass and make the prayer for breaking the fast.

Ingredients

- 7 dates, soaked
- 237ml/8oz/1 cup milk
- pinch cinnamon or ginger powder (optional)

Main Courses

Biryani

Serves 6-8

Biryani is a dish made from rice with spiced meat or vegetables. The name is derived from the Persian word *berya* which means "fried" or "roasted" because, after some cooking, it's dried off in the oven. There are so many different types of biryani and even in India and Pakistan each province has its own version – there was once a Moghul king who wore a different turban for each type of biryani that he was served!

I was asked to make this dish by a friend of mine for her daughter's pre-marriage (*nikkah*) party who was marrying a Pakistani brother. My Anglo-Asian convert friend warned, "Don't make it too hot, Karimah!" "Hmm", I thought, "Does she really know Pakistanis?" Ignoring her advice, I made it really hot and our new Pakistani friends really loved it. The moral of the tale is adjust your seasonings to the taste of your guests, especially when there's a wedding involved!

Preparation

1 Process the following ingredients in a blender to make a paste: yoghurt, salt, green chillies, garlic, ginger, mint, fresh coriander, tomatoes, ground coriander, ground cumin, chilli powder, ground cloves, ground cinnamon. Spread over the chicken and leave in a covered bowl for at least two hours or better still 24 hours in the fridge.

2 After the meat has marinated, you are ready to make the biryani. Soak the rice in 6 cups of water and set aside. Add a pinch of saffron to 4oz/1/2 cup of milk and set aside to infuse. On a medium heat add the ghee in a large saucepan and fry the cashew nuts, cinnamon, crushed cardamom and cloves for 30 seconds, stirring constantly so that the ghee becomes infused with the spices and the nuts turn golden. Add the sliced onion, and stir until transparent. Add the meat with the marinade to the same saucepan and cook on a medium heat until the meat is completely done, stirring regularly and allowing the moisture to evaporate. This should take 30-60 minutes depending on whether it's chicken or lamb.

3 Rinse and drain the rice again, placing it in a saucepan and cover with cold water, about two centimetres or an inch above the rice. Cook on a high heat for five minutes, then turn down to a low heat and cover for five minutes before turning the heat off. Take the lid off otherwise the rice will cook further. Mix a cup of the cooked rice with the saffron milk, and then mix with the other rice to get saffron streaks. Mixed frozen vegetables could be added at this stage.

4 Layer the rice and then the meat in an oven-safe dish and cover it with foil and then a lid for 90 minutes at 300°F/150°C/Gas Mark 2. Then carefully tip the biryani out on to a large serving plate and garnish with chopped coriander and mint leaves. It can be eaten with Mediterranean salad and yogurt.

Ingredients

- 1kg/2lbs/8 cups chicken or lamb, rinsed and diced
- 235ml/8oz/1 cup yoghurt
- 5ml/1 tsp coarse sea salt
- 5-10 green chillies, minced
- 5ml/1 tsp fresh garlic paste
- 5ml/1 tsp fresh ginger paste
- 10g/2oz/½ cup fresh mint, chopped
- 10g/2oz/½ cup fresh coriander, chopped
- 3 medium-sized tomatoes, chopped
- 5ml/1 tsp ground coriander
- 5ml/1 tsp ground cumin
- 5ml/1 tsp chilli powder
- 5ml/1 tsp ground cloves
- 5ml/1 tsp ground cinnamon
- 480g/25oz/3 cups rice, washed and soaked
- 1 pinch saffron
- 117ml/2oz/½ cup milk
- 15ml/1 tbsp cashews, chopped
- 1 cinnamon stick, broken into bits
- 3 whole cloves
- 5 whole cardamom pods
- 3 medium onions, finely sliced
- 45ml/3 tbsp ghee (or clarified butter)
- 10g/2oz/¼ cup fresh coriander, chopped (for garnish, optional)
- 10g/2oz/¼ cup fresh mint, chopped (for garnish, optional)

Karimah's **Goat Curry**

Serves 4

Practically since birth I've eaten curry: there were even spices in my mother's milk! Throughout my childhood, my Mauritian grandma was the best cook in my world and she set the standard by which my mum's curry was measured and she did a pretty good job. I have eaten curry all over the world, especially when I was a practising Rasta.

Caribbean curry is not like any other curry: the spice blend is distinctive but, as far as hotness goes, this one's on par with a vindaloo, and is made in a similar way by marinating the goat meat hours beforehand. You can buy Caribbean curry powder from the shops although it's not as good the homemade version.

Preparation

1 Wash the meat in water with salt or sprinkle lemon juice over the meat, spread over with clean hands then rinse off with lots of water and drain. Add the onion, salt, pepper, and thyme to the meat. Shred the scotch bonnet peppers into small pieces using a knife and fork; you must protect your hands as the pepper can burn sensitive skin, including if you touch your eyes or lips afterwards. Hot pepper sauce is an alternative to scotch bonnet peppers. Add the shredded pepper to the meat and spices and toss with a large fork or spoon. Cover with cling film and leave in a cool place (less than 10°C) for at least three hours, or, even better, overnight.

2 When ready to cook, put the vegetable oil in large pot and put on a medium heat. Add the marinated meat and stir every few minutes to brown it on all sides and to caramelise the onions. In the meantime, put the stock cube and coconut cream into heat proof jug and add two cups of boiling water to dissolve them. Add the curry powder to the meat and stir, and turn the heat down to medium-low to cook spices into the meat but not to burn them. Add the dissolved stock mixture to the pot and add the remaining cup of boiling water. Simmer on medium-low heat for 30 minutes with a lid on.

3 While the meat is simmering, prepare the potatoes (3cm/1⅕″ cubes) and add to the fully simmered meat mixture. Turn the heat up to medium so that the potatoes boil for 15minutes, then turn the hob down to low for another 15minutes, until the potatoes are slightly soft when tested with a knife. Use a fork to break up some of the potatoes against the sides of the pot to thicken the gravy.

4 For true Caribbean style, serve with delicious rice and peas, plantain and coleslaw.

Ingredients

- 500g/18oz/4 cups goat meat or mutton
- 1 large onion, sliced
- 5 cloves garlic, crushed
- 1 large bay leaf
- 5ml/1 tsp seas salt
- 5ml/1 tsp black pepper
- 5ml/1 tsp dried thyme
- 30ml/2 tbsp Caribbean curry powder
- 1-2 scotch bonnet peppers, shredded
- 15ml/1 tbsp West Indian hot pepper sauce
- 500g/1lb/4 cups potatoes, peeled and diced
- 1 stock cube
- 10-20g/½oz/1 tbsp coconut cream
- 700ml/25oz/3 cups boiling water
- 30ml/2 tbsp vegetable oil

Faith **Roast Chicken**

Serves 4-6

This is the second part of the two-from-one-chicken dishes, which is great to avoid expense and waste; the first part was Faith Chicken Soup in the soup section. So after you have poached the chicken in seasoned water you can season it further by adding ingredients like prunes, apricots, and root vegetables before roasting. This version uses prunes and almonds to give it that taste of North Africa.

Preparation

1 While the chicken is cooling (see the recipe above for Faith Chicken Soup), gently blend together the olive oil, cumin, coriander, chilli, cinnamon, honey, garlic, and lemon juice in a cup or glass. Use clean hands or a spoon to wipe this marinade over the chicken without disturbing it, e.g. the legs or wings. Add 2 to 3 cups of pitted prunes, according to taste, and cover the baking dish with foil or a lid if appropriate and place it in preheated oven Gas Mark 7/425°F/220°C for 20 minutes.

2 Take the dish out of oven and remove the lid or foil and baste the chicken with juices, spooning the juices from the bottom of the pan over the breast and legs of the bird before returning it to the oven, and put the foil or lid back on. Turn the temperature down to Gas Mark 3/325°F/160°C for another 30 minutes for a small chicken and 45 minutes a large chicken. Then take the dish out of the oven remove lid and return it to the oven for another 10-15 minutes to crisp up the skin.

3 When done, the chicken can be served in a ceramic dish or tagine with bread and an accompanying salad. Or it can be placed on a bed of couscous or quinoa, with the gravy in a jug to accompany the roast chicken as well as a side salad.

Ingredients

- 15ml/1 tbsp olive oil
- 10ml/2 tsp ground cumin
- 10ml/2 tsp ground coriander
- 5ml/1 tsp chilli powder
- 2/½ml/½ tsp ground cinnamon
- 15ml/1 tbsp honey
- 3 cloves of crushed garlic
- 30ml/2 tbsp lemon juice
- 235g/4oz/1 cup pitted prunes
- Roasted sliced almonds for dressing

Did you know?

Prunes are great anti-oxidants that aid digestion, lower cholesterol and help to prevent heart attacks. Okra has great medicinal qualities in soothing stomach complaints.

Jollof Rice

Serves 6

Jollof Rice is a delicious and popular dish made in many West African countries. Most of the ingredients are readily available in most shops and markets these days! Its origin however could be a case for the African League of Nations as it's even eaten in East Africa too, in Somalia, as my sister Layla tells me. It's an African version of biryani: there are many variations but this is mine!

Preparation

1 Wash the lamb in salt water, rinse, drain and season with salt and pepper. Cover and allow to stand for 1-2 hours in the fridge or cool place at less than 10°C/50°F. Heat the oil in a saucepan and fry the meat on medium to high heat until brown on all side; it should take 10-15 minutes. Remove the lamb and set aside in a bowl. Blend the onions, garlic, ginger, chillies, tomatoes, and tomato paste in a blender and add to the same saucepan on a medium heat for five minutes and then turn the heat down for a further 5 minutes, thereafter adding the meat back to the sauce.

2 Drain the rice and stir well into the lamb tomato mixture. Add salt and pepper and, if you wish, the thyme. Stir in 250ml/8 fl oz of stock or hot water with three dissolved stock cubes. Then add enough cold water to cover the rice if needed – one fingertip above the level of the rice (about two centimetres or just under an inch). Turn heat up high for five minutes to bring to the boil and then turn down very low and cover, cooking for another 15-20 minutes until rice is tender. Test the softness of the rice by tasting it: use a fork to lift out a few grains and taste it. Serve hot, garnished with parsley or fresh coriander and serve with an accompanying salad.

Ingredients

- 500g/1 lb/4 cups lamb shoulder, diced
- 15ml/½oz/1 tbsp vegetable oil
- 3 large onions, finely chopped
- 5 cloves garlic, peeled and finely chopped
- 1-3 chillies (scotch bonnet peppers), finely chopped
- 5ml/1 tsp dried thyme (optional)
- 235ml/8oz/1 cup tomatoes, chopped
- 45ml/3 tbsp/¼ cup tomato paste
- 250g/8oz/1 cup frozen mixed vegetables
- 150g/5oz/1 cup mushrooms, sliced
- 500g/1 lb/3 cups long-grain rice, washed and soaked
- 5ml/1 tsp salt
- 5ml/1 tsp black pepper
- 1L/1 quart/4 cups stock
- Fresh parsley or coriander for garnish

Karimah's **Chicken Korma**

Serves 4-6

This mild curry has its roots in the cuisine of the Moghul Empire which was influenced by subtle Persian and Turkish flavours. It's a dish of braised, stewed meat in a nutty yogurt or creamy sauce; and is a great curry to introduce the uninitiated into the curry club. I have added okra to it for texture and health reasons, and it's great for people are fasting or ladies who are pregnant.

Preparation

Wash and drain the diced chicken. Blend all spices (except the bay leaves) and the yogurt together in the bowl and then add the chicken. Cover with cling film and leave to marinate in a cool place (at less than 10°C/50°F) for at least an hour but not for more than 48 hours. Once the chicken is marinated and you are ready to cook, fry the chopped onions and garlic in the oil until golden. Then add the chicken and cook on a low to medium heat for 20 minutes, stirring every five minutes. You will see chicken begin to release juices, making a gravy. Add the coconut milk and water and cook for a further five minutes. Then add the crushed almonds and raisins, and turn down low to simmer for another 15 minutes. Finally add the okra and cook a further 10 minutes on a low heat. Garnish with fresh coriander, and serve with either wholemeal rice or brown pitta with an accompanying salad.

Ingredients

- 1kg/2⅕lbs/8 cups chicken breast, diced
- 3 onions, finely chopped
- 3 cloves garlic
- 20ml/1 heaped tbsp fresh ginger, finely grated
- 150g/5oz/¾ cup plain thick yogurt
- 15ml/1 tbsp vegetable oil
- 100g/4oz/1 cup okra, topped and tailed
- 45g/1½oz/3 tbsp ground almonds
- 5ml/1 tsp turmeric
- 5ml/1 tsp ground coriander
- 5ml/1 tsp salt
- 5ml/1 tsp black pepper
- 1 dried chilli
- 5ml/1 tsp garam masala
- 5 crushed cardamoms
- 2 bay leaves
- Pinch of saffron (optional)
- 235ml/8oz/1 cup/1 tin coconut milk
- 511ml/18 fl oz/4 cups of cold water
- 100g/3½oz/½ cup raisins optional
- some coriander leaves, finely chopped to garnish
- ½ lemon, juiced

Moroccan **Couscous** with **Lamb** and **Vegetables**

Serves 6-8

As a convert to Islam I was invited by my local Moroccan community to eat this Friday afternoon treat. There was a large mountain of vegetables on a soft fluffy bed of couscous, but where was the meat, I asked myself? But as I dug through the vegetables I got my answer when I finally found the meat. We should be grateful for the food Allah gives us so long as it's halal and wholesome. There is wisdom in this because it's always best to eat fruits, salads and vegetables first before you eat meat or fish. Some Moroccans like white couscous but I prefer the more Islamic wholemeal couscous that you can now buy in most supermarkets. It's better for the digestion and in the long term better for your health. I love this one-bowl meal, served with gravy and a spicy hot onion chutney: what more could you want after Friday prayers?

Did you know?

Lean lamb is a good source of iron. Chickpeas are a good source of protein, fibre, and phytoestrogens.

Preparation

1 Place the couscous in a large serving bowl, add salt and pepper and the lukewarm water, cover and set aside for three minutes. Then add the olive oil, and gradually work the three remaining cups of water into the couscous with clean hands, tossing it and rubbing the grains between your palms. Leave to stand while you prepare the lamb and vegetables.

2 Heat the oil in a pan or couscoussier (a saucepan with steamer section on top). Add the lamb on a high heat to brown it, then reduce the heat to medium and add the onions and garlic and cook them until golden. Add the spices and all ingredients, except chickpeas, stir then cover and simmer for about 20 minutes. Add the chickpeas and heat through for 5 minutes.

3 Place the steamer section on top of the couscoussier and take a handful of rehydrated couscous and generously sprinkle around the steamer leaving the middle section clear. Put the lid on and leave for five minutes. The steam of the cooking lamb and vegetables will steam the couscous. Repeat the process every five minutes until all the couscous is inside the steamer, and leave to steam for a further 10 minutes with lid on.

4 Serve the couscous in a large communal bowl and add the lamb in the centre and cover with the vegetables. Eating couscous the Moroccan way means that you eat the vegetables first which is wonderful for the digestion. The sauce may be evenly poured over the central section and any excess can be placed on the table in a serving jug. Traditionally Moroccan couscous is also served with a hot onion, raisin and cinnamon salsa.

Ingredients

- 500g/1 lb/4 cups lamb (neck or shoulder), diced
- 10ml/2 tsp olive oil
- 2 cloves garlic, chopped
- 1 onion, chopped
- 10ml/2 tsp ground cinnamon
- 10ml/2 tsp paprika
- 10ml/2 tsp turmeric
- 10ml/2 tsp ground ginger
- 10ml/2 tsp black pepper
- pinch saffron
- 440g/15½oz/1 can peeled tomatoes, with juice
- 235ml/8oz/1 cup water
- 15ml/1 tbsp tomato puree
- 75g/3oz/1 cup carrots, chopped
- 75g/3oz/1 cup swedes, chopped
- 75g/3oz/1 cup squash, chopped
- 75g/3oz/1 cup courgettes, chopped
- 15ml/1 tbsp each sultanas
- 15ml/1 tbsp dried apricots, chopped
- 15ml/1 tbsp almonds, chopped
- 10ml/½oz/½ cup fresh parsley
- 10ml/½oz/½ cup fresh coriander
- 300g/10oz chickpeas, freshly cooked or canned

For the couscous
- 2 cups wholemeal couscous
- 2 cups lukewarm water
- 15ml/1 tbsp olive oil
- 5ml/1 tsp salt
- 5ml/1 tsp ground black pepper

Persian **Chicken Stew** in **Pomegranate** and **Walnut**

Serves 4

It's a sweet and sour dish that I first remember was made for me by a friend's mum who had come to the UK from Tehran to fast during Ramadan. I fell in love with this dish and like with many other Persian creations, this particular love affair continues. This rich chicken stew, made with walnut and pomegranate syrup; known as *Khoresh-e fesenjan* is a famous and memorable Persian dish that is usually prepared for festive occasions like Eid. This dish is not as difficult as some princesses make it out to be and my recipe has the seal of approval from the Prince of Persia himself! What else can I say but alhamdulilah!

Preparation

1 Heat the olive oil in a large, heavy deep-sided frying pan over medium heat. Cook and quickly brown the chicken on all sides. Remove from pan, and set aside. Besides chicken breasts, you could use a whole chicken chopped up or thighs instead. Place the onion in the pan and fry until golden and translucent, then add the cinnamon, cardamom, saffron and ground walnuts. Cook on a medium heat for 5-10 minutes to allow the walnuts to release their oil. Return the chicken to the pan with the onions and walnuts, and blend in the pomegranate syrup. Reduce the heat to low, cover, and simmer on a very low heat for an hour so that the flavours infuse into the flesh, stirring occasionally. If you have the time it is better to make this dish the day before and refrigerate it, then warming it up so that the meat becomes really infused with flavour.

2 Serve with basmati rice, raw spring onions, fresh tarragon on the stems and whole radishes. The sweet flavours of the dish are balanced by the fresh, sharp taste of the onions, radish and fresh herbs.

Ingredients

- 4 skinless, boneless chicken breast halves
- 30ml/2 tbsp/¼ cup olive oil
- 1 large onion, finely chopped
- 115-200g/4-7oz/1-2 cups ground walnuts (to taste)
- 15ml/1 tbsp tomato puree
- 240-480ml/8-16oz/1-2 cups pomegranate paste or syrup (to taste)
- 5ml/1 tsp ground cinnamon
- 5ml/1 tsp saffron strands
- 5ml/1 tsp ground cardamom
- 2.5ml/½ tsp nutmeg (optional)

Did you know?

The Prophet, peace be upon him, said, "He who has eaten garlic should not come to our mosque." (Bukhari and Muslim) The same is true of raw onion as well, so a handful of fennel seeds eaten on the way to the mosque serves to sweeten the breath and eases the stomach.

Karimah's **Turkish Bamiya**

Serves 2 as a main and 4 as side dish

While researching recipes for this book, I came across various Middle Eastern bamiya dishes. Bamiya, which we know as okra or ladies' fingers, is great for the stomach, arthritis, diabetes and pregnant women. In Ramadan, its laxative properties and other amazing nutrients are really beneficial too!

I usually eat bamiya in Lebanese restaurants which is served with a mild tomato sauce but recently I've came across an eighteenth-century Ottoman recipe that uses pomegranate puree instead of tomatoes. I felt a bit short changed because I'm a girl that loves my pomegranate sauce and some of the restaurants tend to overcompensate for what they think are unadventurous British palates which are in fact a lot more sophisticated and adventurous than some might think. This recipe combines the best of both worlds and insha'Allah will give you great pleasure.

Preparation

1 Wash the meat in salty water, and drain, then marinate it in the salt, pepper, cinnamon, tossing the meat so that the spices cover all of it. While the meat is marinating, prepare the onions and garlic and set them aside. In a medium-sized saucepan add the butter and warm on a medium-high heat. After a couple of minutes add the meat cubes and brown them on all sides; the meat may stick at first but will loosen as it browns, and this helps seal in the flavour of the meat and the marinade. Then turn heat down to low to medium and add the onions and let them turn a translucent golden colour then add the crushed garlic and cook for further three minutes taking care that the garlic doesn't burn. Then add the tomato puree. Prepare the okra (and if you prefer cut it into smaller pieces which will make the sticky juices come out when you're cooking) and add it to the pot. Then add pomegranate juice and stir it in gently. Finally add the water. Turn heat up and bring the mixture to the boil and then turn it down low to simmer for 15 minutes. Cover the pot with a lid to keep the moisture in while simmering.

2 Serve as a side dish as part of mezze or as a main course with either bread or rice, drizzle with olive oil and lemon juice, if you like, for a real Middle Eastern flavour.

Ingredients

- 500g/18oz/2½ cups lamb or beef neck, diced into small pieces
- 300g/11oz okra, topped and tailed and chopped.
- 3 small onions, chopped
- 15ml/1 tbsp butter or vegetable oil
- 3 cloves garlic, crushed
- 15ml/1 tbsp tomato puree
- 5ml/1 tsp salt
- 5ml/1 tsp black pepper
- 5ml/1 tsp cinnamon
- 15ml/1 tbsp pomegranate syrup
- 120ml/4 fl oz/½ cup water

Mrs Curry's
Chicken Vindaloo

Serves 4

As the cultural exchange in Muslim London continues, Moroccans now are learning to make curry and Pakistanis are learning to make harira soup! I have a "sis-star" friend who is Moroccan and her husband loves curry, he is a pepper addict and loves curry so much, the hotter the better, and so for this reason we call him Mr Curry.

This chicken vindaloo recipe is dedicated to his wife, my good friend, whose family embraced me as a new Muslim and taught me so much about the Muslim way, may Allah bless them all, amen!

Vindaloo is a very hot curry that originated in Goa, India. The word "vindaloo" originates from when the Portuguese were in India and "carne de vinha d'alhos" meant "meat with wine and garlic". The dish evolved into a curry when the Goan Indians gave it their special treatment, substituting the wine with vinegar and adding plenty of aromatic South Asian spices. It is also a curry without tomatoes that is traditionally made by marinating the meat or seafood and so it can be prepared in the morning or even the night before. For a winter version of this dish, I have decided to add extra chilli, ginger and turmeric to help fight the cold and to get those sinuses flowing.

Preparation

1 Leave the chicken to soak in a bowl of water with one tablespoon of salt and two tablespoons of lemon juice for 15-20 minutes, then rinse or drain. Grind the cloves, cardamom pods, bay leaves, mustard seeds and cinnamon stick using a mortar and pestle (or coffee grinder or mini chopper). Chop two onions and the garlic and puree them into a paste; a Kenwood mini chopper is ideal.

2 Put the chicken in a large enough bowl and add the onion and garlic paste, and all the spices including mustard seeds, cinnamon, vinegar and coriander. Using your hands, or a large spoon if you are squeamish, mix the chicken with the other ingredients so it is fully covered. Cover the bowl with lid or cling film and marinate for at least four hours (in a fridge or in a cool place that is less than 10°C/50°F).

3 When the chicken has marinated, heat all the ghee in a large saucepan and slice the remaining onion and fry it on a medium heat, stirring occasionally until it is golden. Stir the marinated chicken in with the onions, and keep it on medium heat for ten minutes to brown the chicken pieces. Cover the saucepan and turn it down low for 45 minutes, so that the chicken will release its natural juices, but remain tender after it is cooked. The lid must be tight fitting so that the juices and evaporating fluid are kept in the saucepan and not let out as steam. This will make the gravy, as otherwise you will end up with a dry curry and maybe even a burnt one! Serve with boiled rice and a selection of salads – salsa cebolla is great as is rainbow salad. Insha'Allah, you too can join the curry club.

Ingredients

- 1½kg/2½lbs/5 cups chicken pieces
- 5ml/1 tsp mustard seeds
- 3 cloves garlic, chopped
- 3 large onions
- 15ml/3 tsp turmeric
- 10ml/2 tsp ground ginger
- 1 cinnamon stick
- 7 green cardamom pods
- 3 bay leaves
- 10ml/2 tsp cumin
- 1 tsp extra hot chili powder
- 10 fresh green chilies
- 20ml/1 cup fresh coriander, chopped
- 5 cloves garlic, chopped
- 25ml/2½ tbsp vinegar
- 5ml/1 tsp salt
- 90g/3¼oz ghee

Marinades

Karimah's **BBQ Marinade**

Enough for 2 large chickens or 20 drumsticks

My earliest memories of the barbeque are quite boring. Long ago in Essex, barbequing was a thing people in America or Australia did and we just heard about it or saw it on that Australian soap, Neighbours. This particular recipe is inspired by the chef and food warrior Jamie Oliver; I had to change the recipe a bit so Jamie wouldn't be knocking on my door, although as he's from Essex like me he would be most welcome, as long as I had a *mahram*.

You can make this marinade even a couple of weeks before and keep it in the fridge. Let's say you want to do a barbeque the next day, say for *iftar* (the meal for breaking the fast), marinade your meat the night before and leave it covered in the fridge and then grill, roast or barbeque it before serving.

Most of the ingredients can be easily obtained from your local halal supermarket; smoky paprika can be bought from some large supermarkets and also in Portuguese shops, in places like Portobello Road in West London, where large Portuguese communities live harmoniously side by side with their Moroccan neighbours.

Preparation

1 Grind all the dry ingredients together – the cloves, fennel, cinnamon, cumin, bay leaves, thyme, black pepper, salt and smoked paprika – using a mortar and pestle or grinder, and then add it to smoothie maker or jug processor. Break the garlic bulb by hand and put all of in except the internal stem. Then add the lemon or orange juice, ketchup or puree and vinegar and turn the machine on for a whole minute, making sure that the garlic bulb has broken down and blended in. Then add the honey or syrup and pulse for 30 seconds; add the olive oil and blend for another 30 seconds. Pour the marinade into an airtight bottle and refrigerate until needed; it will keep for a couple of weeks in the fridge.

2 To use, pour the marinade over cleaned meat and toss so that the meat is well covered. Place in a lidded plastic container and seal or wrap well with clean cling film, making sure no mixture is outside the container. When you work cleanly there is less risk of any infection from uncooked meat juices. Leave to marinate for at least three hours in fridge, and then roast, grill or barbeque thereafter. Chicken wings take about 20 minutes on the barbeque or 40 minutes in a preheated oven (200°C/400°F/Gas 6). Chicken thighs take 50 minutes in the oven or 25 minutes on a barbeque or grill; deboned chicken breast takes 30 minutes to roast and 15 minutes to grill or barbeque. As you can see grilling or barbequing are quicker methods of cooking

Ingredients

- 5 cloves
- 5ml/1 tsp ground cumin
- 5ml/1 tsp ground cinnamon
- 30ml/2 tbsp fennel seeds
- 15ml/3 tsp black pepper
- 5ml/1 tsp sea salt
- handful fresh rosemary or 5ml/1 tsp dried rosemary
- 5 bay leaves
- 5ml/1 tsp of thyme
- 1 garlic bulb
- orange or lemon zest
- 25ml/5 tsp smoked paprika
- 240ml/1 cup balsamic or apple cider vinegar
- 30ml/2tbsp orange or lemon juice
- 3-5 green fresh chillies (optional)
- 120ml/4oz/½ cup honey or golden syrup
- 480ml/4oz/2 cups organic ketchup or 5 tbsp of tomato puree
- 120ml/4oz/½ cup olive oil

Chilli Marinade

This marinade has a Mediterranean vibe about it with a kick of chilli in it for good measure.

Preparation

Mix all the ingredients together and pour over lamb chops or chicken pieces, cover with foil, then with cling film or put in a lidded plastic container and leave in the fridge until ready to grill, fry or barbeque.

Ingredients

- 5ml/1 tsp chilli powder
- 15ml/1 tbsp minced shallot or red onion
- 5ml/1 tsp minced/crushed garlic
- 30g/1oz/½ cup coriander
- 10ml/2 tsp dry oregano
- 5ml/1 tsp cumin
- 120ml/4oz/½ cup lemon juice
- 120ml/4oz/½ cup olive oil
- 5ml/1 tsp salt
- 10ml/2 tsp black pepper

Did you know?

Marinades have been a way of tenderising and preserving meat for years before fridges were invented: the combination of spices and acids like lemon or vinegar help to preserve the freshness of the meat or fish. These marinades are useful if you are going to work or would like to prepare enough food for a few days. Marinated meat can only be left in the fridge for up to 1-3 days, and fish for 24 hours.

Teriyaki Marinade

Preparation

Mix together all the ingredients, pierce holes in the chicken pieces using a sharp knife or skewer and pour over the marinade over the chicken pieces or alternatively seafood like prawns, and cover with foil. Place in a lidded plastic container or cover with cling film and leave in the fridge until ready to grill, fry or barbeque.

Ingredients

- 235ml/8oz/1 cup fresh or tinned pineapple and juice
- 120ml/4oz/½ cup soy sauce
- 15ml/1 table spoon crushed fresh ginger
- 2.5 ml/½ tsp of 5 spice powder
- 60ml/2oz/¼ cup organic cider vinegar
- 5ml/1 tsp black pepper
- 5ml/½ tsp salt

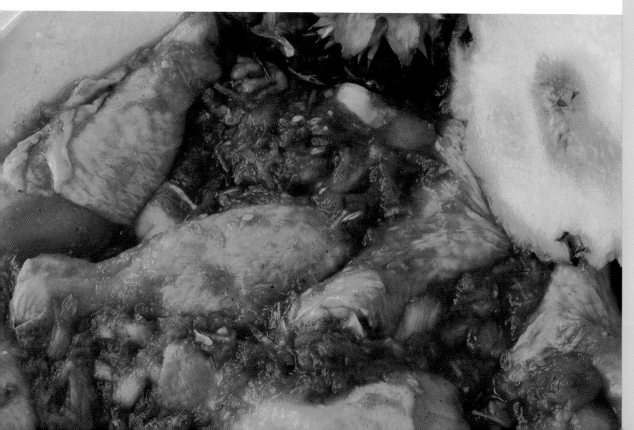

Moroccan Marinade

This marinade is a staple in the fridge of any Moroccan woman who loves cooking!

Preparation

Wash and drain the herbs, I do this by hanging them upside down from hooks after washing and placing rubber band back on to hold the bunches together. Using a food processor, coarsely chop the herbs, peel the garlic and blend all ingredients in a food processor. Store in a lidded glass jar in the fridge. This marinade can be used to marinate meat or chicken.

Ingredients

- 1 bunch coriander
- 1 bunch flat leaf parsley
- 1 bulb garlic
- 120ml/4oz/½ cup Moroccan olive oil
- 15ml/1 tbsp coarse sea salt

Sweets

Lazy Days Apple Pie

Serves 4-6

This quick sweet treat is a simple no-fuss apple pie, and is a useful way to use up all those apples that are not crisp enough to eat. Served with custard, it's a comforting ending to a day of fasting. I was with a Somali friend recently and he said that Somalis like to eat cake and custard later on in the evening after fasting and that they make the best cake in the world. It's wonderful that each culture thinks their cooking is the best and have nostalgic memories of how things used to be cooked back home. The world is now a small place with a jubilant cultural exchange happening wherever you go, so I'd like to think that my Somali brother would love this pie, insha'Allah!

Preparation

1 Preheat the oven to 200°C/400°F/Gas Mark 6. Using a little of the butter and either kitchen tissue or foil from the butter packet, grease a flat baking tray which is big enough to take a 30cm/12" circle of pastry. Add the butter and flour together and mix with your fingertips until it looks like crumbs. Add the egg yolk and a little water to bind the pastry together until it becomes a ball of dough. Sprinkle some more flour on to your work surface and knead the pastry for a few minutes. Using a rolling pin, roll the ball out flat until it forms a 30cm/12" circle, although it doesn't have to be perfect round. Carefully lift and place on the flat baking tray.

2 Get a big bowl and chop the washed apples into it, putting the cores into your kitchen waste for recycling. Pour lemon juice over the apple pieces to stop them going brown. Add the spices – ginger, cinnamon, nutmeg, and mixed spice – and toss them into the apples. Then add the raisins to the apple mix and toss again to make sure that the spices and raisins are evenly mixed with the apples. Add half of the Demerara sugar to the mix and set the other half aside.

3 Now pour the apple mix into the centre of your pastry ring, leaving a 10cm/4" border of pastry around the edges. Fold up the edges of pastry with your hands to cover the fruits, gently scrunching and pleating the pastry together. Remember this is the lazy way, so it's meant to look very rustic rather than perfect: you are just making a package to keep the fruit in while it bakes, making sure to leave a hole in the top, for any steam to escape. Brush the remaining egg white over the pie and sprinkle with remaining brown sugar and then, if you like, add the almonds. Cover the hole with aluminium foil and place in the oven. Cook for 30-35 minutes until the pastry is golden brown. Serve with custard, cream or ice cream.

Ingredients

- 225g/8oz/2 cups plain wholemeal flour
- 15ml/1 tbsp castor sugar
- 5ml/1 tsp ginger powder
- 5ml/1 tsp ground cinnamon
- 5ml/1 tsp mixed spice
- 1 pinch nutmeg
- 150g/5oz/⅔ cup margarine
- 1 large egg, separated white and yolk
- 450g/1 lb/2 cups cooking apples
- 30ml/2tbsp lemon juice
- 115g/4oz/⅔ cup raisins or sultanas
- 75g/3oz/½ cup Demerara brown sugar
- 25g/1oz/¼ cup sliced almonds

Lemon Polenta Cake

Serves 8-12

Making cake is the first thing my Mauritian grandma taught me in the kitchen, and she even gave me three large solid silver forks to mix it with, we didn't use a whisk back then but just plain old elbow grease. This is one of my favourite cakes as it doesn't have too much wheat flour, and it's light and fluffy with a just hint of lemon to stimulate your palate.

Preparation

1. You will need a couple of measuring jugs, a 1.2 litre or 2 pint cake tin or ring, a whisk and ideally a lemon juicer for this recipe. Preheat the oven to Gas Mark 4/180°C/360°F, and grease the cake tin with a little oil on piece of kitchen tissue or using a baking brush.

2. Sift the polenta, flour, salt, and baking powder into a bowl. Put the yogurt, lemon zest, lemon juice and oil into a jug and stir together. Separate the eggs and the egg whites and beat the egg whites in large jug or bowl, adding the three small whole eggs and blending them in softly as you don't want to lose the fluffiness of the whites and then fold in the sugar while the mixture is still fluffy and creamy. Then softly fold yogurt mixture in. Finally add all dry ingredients into the cake mixture in the large bowl, gently blending. Then carefully put the cake batter into the greased cake tin or ring.

Bake for 40-45 minutes or until a skewer comes out cleanly when put through to the bottom of the cake; if the skewer comes out smeared the cake will need longer in the oven. Once done, take the cake out and leave to cool. Don't leave it in the oven, as even when the oven is turned off it can still burn, as a friend of mine found out! Serve with yogurt or crème fraiche and seasonal berries.

Ingredients

- 175g/6oz/¾ cup polenta
- 60g/2oz/¼ cup plain flour
- 7½ml/1½ tsp baking powder
- 2½ml/½ tsp salt
- 75ml/5 tbsp/⅓ cup natural yogurt
- 75ml/5 tbsp/⅓ cup vegetable/sunflower/ground nut oil
- zest, finely grated, of 2 unwaxed lemons
- 30ml/2 tbsp juice of lemon juice
- 3 small whole eggs
- 3 small egg whites
- 200g/7oz/1 cup castor sugar
- yogurt and berries, to accompany

Poetic Pancakes

Serves 2-6

As a convert to Islam, old habits sometimes die hard and so resisting the urge to eat pancakes on Shrove Tuesday is one of them! But when the Muslim hip-hop duo Poetic Pilgrimage flagged up on Facebook that International Women's Day and Pancake Day fell on the same day, I sighed and thought, "Oh well, I suppose I should go and put spice to batter and whip up some pancakes". Inspired by this gentle nudge from the poets, here is my offering. These fragrant flavoursome pancakes are a little bit "Moor" fancy than the typical French ones and can also be eaten with lemon and sugar.

Preparation

1. Mix all ingredients together: first the eggs then the flour, then the spices, and finally the milk and water. Use a whisk to blend all ingredients into a smooth batter; an electric whisk is easier. In a small frying pan add half a teaspoon of oil and, using a kitchen or pastry brush, wipe the oil around the pan. Then pour a quarter cup of batter into the pan and spread the batter around by tilting the pan so that the entire base of the pan is covered. Cook gently on a medium heat for one minute. Using a spatula, gently lift the sides of the pancake, and let it down again, as the centre will always take a bit longer. Turn it over and cook on other side: there's no need to add extra oil, you don't want too much cholesterol do you? With small pancakes it's easy to turn them over using a spatula. After a minute lift one side and flip over to check the colour. Depending on how you like it you can take it off, leaving it more pale, or keep it on for another minute to make it more crispy and golden. The way you layer the pancakes and the fillings you decide to use is up to you. Here are some interesting combinations.

2. For savoury fillings you could use: baked beans sprinkled with cheese; curried beans with yogurt on the side; humus with salad on the side; mayonnaise spread over with smoked salmon and topped with rocket or watercress; and coronation chicken and salad. For sweet fillings, sugar and fresh lemon juice; chocolate spread and sliced bananas; fresh berries and cream; crème fraiche, honey and pistachios; and stewed fruit such as apple or rhubarb with custard. All the possibilities are there, so isn't time you spiced your life up? Ooh la la!

Ingredients

- 240g/8oz/1 cup wholemeal or rice flour
- 1 large egg
- 120ml/4oz/½ cup dairy/ soya milk
- 120ml/4oz/½ cup water
- a pinch of ginger, cinnamon, mixed spice (for sweet ones) or
- a pinch of cumin, coriander, chilli, salt and pepper (for savoury ones)

Suhour Emergency Cake

Serves 8-12

It's a heavy cake-like bread pudding or pound cake: those English and American converts to Islam will know what I mean. It's not a soft and fluffy airy-fairy sort of cake. It's packed with nuts, dates and bananas, so I thought it would be a great thing to eat if you get up late for suhour and need to eat something nutritious in a hurry. Or you could wrap a slice or two and take it to work to break the fast with a glass of milk or juice. This cake packs a punch and a couple of slices should get you through the day, insha'Allah. It's ideal for using up bananas that you've kept a bit too long.

Preparation

1 Preheat the oven to Gas Mark 4/180°C/350°F. Grease a 2lb (21.5 x 11 x 7cm or 8½" x 4¼" x 2¾") and grease the loaf tin with a little oil or butter with a piece of kitchen tissue. Mash the bananas with a fork in a bowl. In a separate bowl cream the butter and sugar together and mix in the eggs, then mix the mashed banana into the butter and cream. Then mix in the flour, cinnamon and mixed spice. Then add the nuts and dates; you should note that the nuts and dates tend to make the mixture really thick, so thick you may not even be able to use an electric whisk to blend the mixture at this stage. Finally add half a cup of milk and mix by hand with a large wooden spoon, then add the remaining ½ cup of milk, doing the same.

2 Scrape the batter into the greased loaf tin and bake for 40 minutes, then lower the temperature to Gas Mark 2/150°C/300°F and cook for a further 30-60 minutes. At this stage, keep testing the cake with a skewer; if it comes out reasonably cleanly after being left in for 30 seconds, then it is ready to take out of the oven. Leave it to cool in the tin for a while before you turn it out on to a rack so that the air can circulate around it. When completely cool, sprinkle with icing sugar and slice and eat. You serve it cold with custard or with a glass of milk before you begin fasting. Remember to make the prayer before fasting insha'Allah, you'll make it through the day with loads of energy.

Ingredients

- 120g/4oz/½ cup butter or margarine
- 100g/4oz/½ cup sugar
- 240g/8oz/1 cup self-raising flour
- 2 large eggs
- 2 very ripe bananas
- 14 dates, stoned and chopped
- 50g/2oz/½ cup pecan nuts, crushed
- 150g/5oz/1½ cup walnuts, crushed
- 5ml/1 tsp ground cinnamon
- 5ml/1 tsp mixed spice powder (nutmeg, clove, aniseed)
- 5ml/1 tsp ground ginger
- 235ml/8oz/1 cup milk

Did you know?

Nutmeg when used in large quantities has an effect on the body that is similar to hashish, and some countries like Saudi Arabia ban its importation unless it constitutes less than 20% of a spice mixture. Some scholars, like Wahba al-Zuhayli, see no harm in using small amounts for flavouring in food.

Karimah's **Bircher Muesli**

Serves 2-4

Muesli is not something common to Arab or Asian culture, but it's something that us European converts are used to and it's packed full of natural energy! I used to eat museli most days on my way to work when I worked as a fashion model in Zurich. This was healthy food on the run, although it's not very Islamic to eat while on the move. This naturally sweet dish combines fruits, nuts and oats to provide a delicious and healthy meal. Created by Dr Bircher-Benner in the 1890s for patients at his Swiss clinic, it's the ideal breakfast in warmer days before the porridge season kicks in. This dish can be prepared the night before or even be made in bulk for three days' supply. It's great for suhour as you just get up open the fridge and stick it in a bowl with yoghurt and honey. I have added some spicy eclectic Karimah touches to bring this muesli into the new millennium.

Preparation

Place the oats and sultanas in a lidded plastic container. Cut the dates open, removing the stones, and checking to make they are free inside of insect eggs and so on. Chop and add them to the oats and sultanas. Then add the spices; cinnamon, ginger and coconut, and finally add the milk, making sure that it is well mixed in. Wash and drain the apple and berries, chopping the apple into small pieces and adding it to the oats immediately otherwise it will go brown. Take any green stems or leaves off the berries, and add them in. Depending on their size halve or quarter the strawberries before adding them. Some people add the fruit at the last minute but proper Swiss muesli has a lovely pink colour from the juice from the berries which is normally infused while soaking into the oats and the milk. Cover with an airtight lid and place in the fridge overnight. When ready to eat, put a portion into a bowl, pour the yoghurt over the top, drizzle with honey and sprinkle with black seeds – and up, up and away!

Ingredients

- 150g/6oz/½ cup dry rolled porridge oats
- 75g/3oz/¼ cup dried sultanas or raisins
- 235ml/8oz/1 cup milk
- 1 apple
- 15ml/1 tbsp desiccated coconut
- 100ml/3oz/½ cup natural yogurt
- 25g/1oz/⅓ cup flaked almonds, toasted
- 150g/6-7oz/1⅓ cups blackberries, strawberries, raspberries
- 5ml/1 tsp ginger
- 5ml/1 tsp cinnamon
- 7 dried stoned dry dates
- 15ml/1 tbsp clear honey
- 15ml/1 tsp black seeds

Index